KNOW YOUR SWING

"Tradition is the nature and backbone of golf. That is the reason that the game is as old as it is and as successful as it is. It is probably the oldest sport, outside of archery maybe. Golf has a history that is Tradition is the nature and backbone of golf. That is the reason that the game is as old as it is and as successful as it is. It is probably the oldest sport, outside of archery maybe. Golf has a history that is predicated on tradition, and without this tradition I don't think this game would be where it is today. It is historically proven that it is probably the most honest game on the planet. A player on a daily occurrence will call a penalty on himself. No other sport in the world that I know of does anything like that."

—*Retired CBS TV golf producer Frank Chirkinian*

"Golf is a great game because of the rules as stated by the Royal and Ancient and by the USGA. You have to guide and you have to rule on yourself. To be able to rule against yourself takes fortitude and integrity."

—*Roger Cleveland*

"These things are the keys—etiquette, sportsmanship, integrity, honesty, calling penalties on yourself. Congratulating the other player when he beats you. These factors have always been the spine of this great game. The top golfers of the world still have these values well intact."

—*Peter Jacobsen*

"You can see tradition in the young golfers, they are very well mannered and very well dressed. They should continue to look at people like Arnold Palmer and Jack Nicklaus. Look at what they have done for the game and how they have stood up for it."

—*Chi Chi Rodriguez*

"Golfers have always had great integrity about the game of golf in every aspect. Being forthright and being honest sum up my interpretation of traditional values."

—*Corey Pavin*

KNOW YOUR SWING

SWING

GLENN MONDAY

McGraw-Hill

New York   Chicago   San Francisco   Lisbon   London   Madrid   Mexico City
Milan   New Delhi   San Juan   Seoul   Singapore   Sydney   Toronto

The McGraw·Hill Companies

Library of Congress Cataloging-in-Publication Data

Monday, Glenn.
    Know your swing / by Glenn Monday.—1st ed.
       p.   cm.
    ISBN 0-07-144910-8
    1. Swing (Golf)   2. Golf—Training.   I. Title.

  GV979.S9M65   2005
  796.352'3—dc22   2004024976

1 2 3 4 5 6 7 8 9 0 FGR/FGR 0 9 8 7 6 5

ISBN 0-07-144910-8

McGraw-Hill books are available at special quantity discounts to use as premiums and sales promotions, or for use in corporate training programs. For more information, please write to the Director of Special Sales, Professional Publishing, McGraw-Hill, Two Penn Plaza, New York, NY 10121-2298. Or contact your local bookstore.

This book is printed on acid-free paper.

CONTENTS

Contents

FOREWORD

As a golf professional myself, I know what it takes to effectively teach the game of golf while conveying the proper methods and teachings.

This book, *Know Your Swing*, written by Los Angeles teaching pro Glenn Monday, is an easy-to-understand explanation of the action of the golf swing.

The author with Bruce Fleisher. Senior PGA Tour player Bruce Fleisher is a past U.S. Amateur champion. He also holds the record for most tournament wins in a three-year span by a professional golfer, a feat he accomplished from 1999 through 2001.

Top pros want a swing that repeats the proper fundamentals. By following the details that Glenn Monday writes about, your swing will be on its way to better and more precise repetition.

Know Your Swing guides you through the fundamentals and provides you with excellent drills that will empower you with the proper feel of a first-class swing.

I have enjoyed being on the driving range with Glenn Monday at many of our tour site stops. On these occasions I discovered his love and knowledge of the game as well as his terrific communication skills.

I congratulate Glenn on his thirty-sixth year as a teaching pro and on his prestigious honor of being named a Top 50 Teacher in the West by *Golf Magazine*.

I endorse the book *Know Your Swing* and am confident you will gain valuable tour player insight.

—Bruce Fleisher, 2001 U.S. Senior Open Champion

ACKNOWLEDGMENTS

Special thanks to the following:

To Arnold Palmer, a true friend to the teaching pro and an inspiration to me.

To my editor, Mark Weinstein, for making this book possible.

Thanks to 2001 U.S. Senior Open champion Bruce Fleisher.

The author with two of golf's greatest legends, "The King," Arnold Palmer, and "The Golden Bear," Jack Nicklaus, at Riviera Country Club, Los Angeles, California.

Acknowledgments

It was a pleasure working with the great actor Efrem Zimbalist Jr. and the extraordinary songwriter Chuck Jackson.

Thanks to PGA Tour players Ken Still, George Archer, Tom Purtzer, Chi Chi Rodriguez, Jim Ferree, Simon Hobday, Al Geiberger, Dan Forsman, and Lanny Wadkins. Also, to all the PGA tournament players who have been generous with their time.

Thanks also to Dave Crawley, Scott Darrough, Mike Edgley, Warren Keating, Tom Marshall, Margo Van, and Lillian Wilkey for their terrific photographs and to Roxanne Benton and Warren Keating for their help with the illustrations.

INTRODUCTION

Having just walked onto the driving range at Rancho Park Golf Course in Los Angeles, it caught my attention that legendary San Francisco quarterback and Senior PGA Tour winner John Brodie was helping eight-time PGA Tour winner Bruce Devlin of Australia.

After listening in on Brodie's instruction, and feeling that I could add to the effectiveness of Bruce's swing, I reached into my pocket and pulled out a crisp hundred-dollar bill. I handed the hundred to Bruce and said, "If I can't help you in five minutes, the hundred is yours."

Hearing my words, Brodie turned to Devlin and said, "If I were you, I'd give that man five minutes." John Brodie pulled up a folding golf chair and sat in to observe my work. When I had finished, Brodie gave me a great compliment.

"You helped him get started in the right direction," he said. "You were able to explain to him why he had to get his grip in a little different position, which allowed him to get the club up the wall and hit the ball where he was aiming. Getting him to do that is very tough. He has struggled—he has put in six years of sheer struggle—and now after your lesson he is hitting the ball better than I have seen in a long time. Now he's enthused. *That* is the biggest thing."

In the same way I helped Bruce Devlin, I have written this book to help you get started in the right direction with your golf swing—to help you to *Know Your Swing*. A golf swing is a well-planned and well-rehearsed target-oriented body motion. When you know the proper route from beginning to finish, you play with confidence. And

The author with Bruce
Devlin.

when your mind and muscles are on the same track, your golf swing holds up under pressure.

I believe for you to have a good golf swing, it has to be perfectly clear in your mind what you are trying to accomplish. You must know before you go. In the upcoming pages I will teach you the golf swing using my winning instruction formula.

Once you understand the action of a golf swing mentally, you will have a pattern to follow, and with each swing you'll try to swing on track. When you know which muscles are required to do a certain action, you will be able to repeat the action until it is memorized by the muscles. Sound understanding of the overall concept will enable you to perform effectively on the fairway.

Muscle memory allows the muscles to perform a desired action on command. Same muscles, same positions. Correct muscle memory will give your golf swing repeatability, and repetition will help you to achieve good timing. Repetition is the mother of skill. U.S. Open champion Tom Kite has stated that the most important part of a golf swing is repeatability. A golf swing takes little more than a second to complete, but the pro on tour spends a lifetime trying to perfect that action. Precision repetition is the goal.

The golf swing is a total body movement. The hands, arms, and legs all play key roles. Throughout this book I will give you solid swing keys that help you to initiate and repeat the movement. Power in the golf swing is generated when all the parts of the body do the right things at the right time. Timing will come to your swing through practice, but you must practice a well-schooled, consistent golf swing.

As a lifelong teaching professional, I believe in a tour-tight approach to the golf swing, with precise, target-oriented body movement throughout. I build a golf swing step-by-step with care. My goal is to teach the art and science of the golf swing in equal parts. A golf swing is most effective when you understand and can duplicate the proper fundamentals. The closer you can come to repeating a sound golf swing, the higher your percentage of good shots will be.

Here is a breakdown of the sequence of action I follow:

1. In the first lesson, I present key concepts to build a good golf swing. Golf being a game of opposites, the left side controls the swing and the right side goes with the flow. I give an overview of the components of the golf swing and introduce the inside-out swing path.

2. We next work out in detail the second half of the swing, impact through finish, establishing balance and control of this crucial split-second movement so that you know the destination of your swing.

3. The backswing and downswing through impact are added next, as you learn to control swing path and maintain the power angle to be released through the ball on impact.

4. In the rehearsal phase, I guide you through each and every motion, fine-tuning as we go. During this time I work only with the left hand, arm, and left side of the body (for right-handed

golfers), teaching the left side to be the leader and the right side to stay relaxed and passive.

5. Next we attach the right hand—but teach you to let it go for the ride. The left side controls and the right side is the passenger during the journey.

6. Leg action: once the golf swing is put together properly from the waist up, I then add the leg action.

7. The final piece is turning the mechanical process into an instinctive smooth motion by adding balance as well as tempo, timing, and rhythm.

After I have introduced the seven steps, I then give you the green light to go practice.

Our result is a fundamentally sound golf swing that repeats, has good tempo, is effective, and holds up under pressure. It will enable you to take a golf swing to the driving range and not have to try to discover one when you get there. Through practice your timing will get better and you will notice that your percentage of good shots will increase. And when that happens, you'll gain more and more confidence on the course.

No Homework

Until you have gone through all seven steps with me, I ask you not to practice, do "homework," think, or do exercises between lessons. I want you to come back to the next lesson just the way you left, so we can go forward with the good and not continue to make the same swing errors between lessons. However, I do suggest that you practice your putting, so the short game can improve while I'm improving your swing.

Phase 4, the rehearsal phase, is the most time-consuming. As I guide you through the various areas of the golf swing, you will get a more familiar feeling for these areas, and become more comfortable going to and being in those areas. I have found that people learn at varying speeds. The way I teach, you can have a good golf swing at or near fifteen hours of instruction, regardless of your skill level. Under normal circumstances with two half-hour lessons a week, you can complete these lessons and go to the driving range in only two and a half to three months from the first lesson. But here is the good part. After eighteen months of practice, you will be playing as well as most people that have been around the game for fifteen years. So, this method is effectively a thirteen-year shortcut to enjoying the great game of golf.

In the following chapters, you will become acutely aware of how each of the significant and critical parts of your body relates to your golf swing. Since the purpose of this book is to build a sound golf swing that will be enjoyed for a lifetime, it is best to start at the beginning. I invite you to follow along as I walk you through each part of the swing. As the saying goes, first you build a racetrack and then you race. So let's go build ourselves a racetrack.

FIRST LESSON: KEY CONCEPTS TO BUILDING A GOOD GOLF SWING

In order to help you progress more rapidly, I will repeat key thoughts in varying forms. This is done for two reasons. First, by repetition, you can more quickly grasp the importance of the thought. Second, by presenting the same information in a variety of ways, it is my hope that one of the ways or some of them together will trigger your understanding and help you to learn faster.

This first lesson has proven very helpful to both my students and to myself. The information distilled in it will enable us to look at the game of golf through the same eyes and therefore have better communication throughout this book. During these lessons, I will paint a picture for you that will allow you to know exactly what to do with the club *before* and *as* you swing it.

In 1995 it was my pleasure to publish an interview with PGA Tour and Senior Tour player Jim Ferree in *Golf Tips* magazine. Jim's father was head pro at Pinehurst No. 2 when he was a youngster. I asked Jim if there was anything his father taught him as a young boy that he carried with him on the tour, to which he replied, "Yes, he sat me down and shared with me the valuable information that golf is a game of opposites, and I still use it today."

In 1993 and well into his sixties, Jim was in the top ten in driving distance on the Senior Tour. He has a great, fundamentally sound golf swing. An example of golf being a game of opposites comes from arguably the world's greatest golfer, Bobby Jones. Bobby was right-handed, but the left side of his body controlled his swing. "The only thing the right arm should do in the golf swing is stay out of it," Jones once said.

The great teaching pro Harvey Penick has also chimed in on this phenomenon. In a notebook entry from April 12, 1924, Penick wrote, "It seems to me that very little about a golf swing is consistent with a student's first concept of it. Almost everything is the opposite."

Other examples of golf being a game of opposites will be presented. When you see a golf swing, look at what is going on with the left side of the body—the hand, arm, shoulder, and back; we can refer to this as the motor of the swing. We will first build up the strength and feel of the motor and fine-tune it before we attach the right hand to the club.

When you see a car go down the road, you see the car, but you don't see what causes the car to move—you don't see the motor. When you see a golf pro swing a club, you see the golf swing, but you don't see the muscles the pro is using to cause the action—you don't see the motor of the swing. Therein lies my job as a teacher. I've got to educate, strengthen, and fine-tune the muscles on the left side.

This first lesson is only an outline of what the left side does during the action of the swing. We will go into details of how you go up to the top of the backswing and how you come down and through the ball in upcoming chapters.

I will give you easy-to-understand checkpoints along the way. These checkpoints will increase your awareness and give you the proper feel for your swing. With this knowledge, you will have the ability to come close to precise repetition.

Now I want to start you out the same way that I begin with all of my students, regardless of their skill level. The intention of the first lesson is to build a good golf swing into your thinking. After that is accomplished, we can put this good thinking into your muscle action. The final product will be that your mind and muscles end up on the same track, and your golf swing will begin to hold up under pressure. I believe it is important that you know before you go, as understanding what you are trying to accomplish is the first step in accomplishing anything.

The Glove Hand: First of Golf's Opposites

3

Most professional golfers are right-handed players, and the vast majority of these right-handed players wear a glove, but only on their left—opposite—hand. Why? What does a glove do for them, and what will a glove do for you? A golf glove acts as adhesion between the grip and your hand to form a stronger bond, to help you hold on better. By wearing the glove on their left hand, these pros are indicating that their left hand is the major gripping hand. They are not wearing a glove on their right hand because they don't want to grip the club too tightly with that hand. If the right hand gets too tight, it's like trying to push a car with the brakes on. It wastes energy. It will break down the strength of the left hand, and then you end up with two weak hands. If you've ever had a club spin in your hands at impact, it was because your right hand was too tight. This caused your left hand to be weak, and the club was off on its own. Therefore, the first thing I want you to put in your thinking is that your left hand is your major gripping hand.

Glove Hand and Left Side Control
1. Glove hand (left hand) is the major gripping hand.
2. Left arm controls the direction and the speed of the swing.

Second, it's your left arm that controls the direction and speed of your swing. What does the right side do? Not too much. The left side is your leader, the right side the follower. The left side controls the swing while the right side goes along for the ride. The left side is your authority and the right side is relaxation. If you have ever seen a good player swing a golf club, the swing looks free, easy, fast, smooth, comfortable, coordinated, and effortless; how do good players look that way? It's because they have a leader and a follower. The left side controls the swing and the right side goes with the flow. You've arrived as a golfer when you have the feeling that your entire right side is being pulled through by your left—when you allow your right side to go with the flow.

Shaping Your Shot

Swing path, the path or direction the clubhead travels through the ball, is another example of golf being a game of opposites. Imagine three lines that run parallel to each other and track toward your target. As you are standing in your start position (see Figure 1.1), the line farthest from you is outside of the ball and the line nearest you is inside of the ball. The ball sits on the middle line, which is your target line. If you stood behind the ball facing the target, the outside line would be right of the ball, and the inside line would be left of the ball (see Figure 1.2).

While we talk about the direction that your clubhead travels through the ball (the swing path), keep in mind that the ball flight that

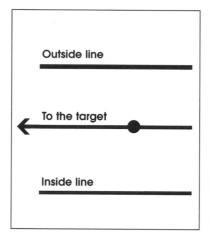

Figure 1.1 Target line, inside and outside lines as seen from the start position (for a right-handed golfcr).

Figure 1.2 Target line, left inside, and right outside lines as seen from behind the ball (for a right-handed golfer).

I am describing requires that the clubface stays looking at the target during the moment of impact.

Let's look at how the direction the clubhead flies through the ball affects ball flight. If your clubhead comes into the ball from outside of the ball and flies inside, your clubhead is traveling left of your target, cutting across the ball, causing it to fly to the right. Remember—*golf is a game of opposites*.

Why does the ball fly right if your clubhead is going left? Because you are putting *spin* on the ball. A golf ball flies according to the spin you put on it, and the spin is the result of the direction the clubhead flies through the ball. If your clubhead approaches the ball from an inside path, your ball flies with the type of spin on it that starts it out to the right, and brings it back to the left (see Figure 1.3).

To what extent you want to spin the ball is related to variances of swing path and clubface position. The first thing you want to learn is to spin the ball slightly from right to left. This is what I'll be teaching you. Once you learn this shot, called the *draw*, the other types of shots become easy. Pros refer to spinning the ball as *shaping your shot* or *flighting your ball*.

U.S. Open champion Corey Pavin says, "I'll aim to the right if I'm trying to draw the ball, but the clubface is always looking at the target. When I'm trying to draw the ball, the clubface will appear to be shut [aimed slightly left of the target] when I'm looking down at it, but it's still looking at the target."

By playing the draw shot, with the clubhead swinging from inside through the ball to outside, you put the type of spin on the ball that

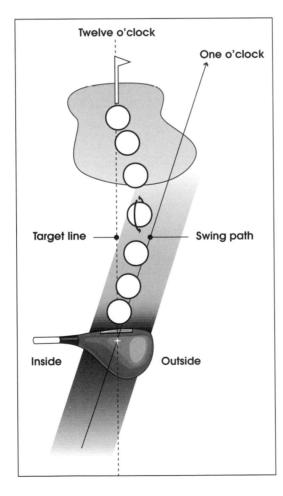

Figure 1.3 The draw shot. Swinging through the ball from an inside path with your clubhead causes it to start out to the right, then brings it back to the left.

The "Shut" Clubhead

When Corey Pavin says his clubface would appear shut (or slightly closed) but in fact be square to the target when hitting a draw shot, it is an illusion that requires explanation to some players. The new player and the unschooled player have a tendency to begin their swings with an open clubface (aimed right of the target). The clubface should instead be closed to the swing path, but square to the target. The look of the correct position takes some getting used to.

allows it to fly farther. The ball becomes more aerodynamic, and when the ball hits the ground, this spin allows it to roll farther. This is why the vast majority of professional players use the inside-out swing path. It is the most successful swing path used by players who know what they are doing. If you don't hit the ball 250 to 300 yards on tour, you don't get much of a paycheck. So the tour players have to take advantage of everything they can to hit the ball as far as they can.

Another reason for an inside-out swing path is you know your ball is going to fly a little left. What does that mean? You eliminate the right side of the golf course and cut out half of the potential trouble. Because most golfers have either never heard of swing path or don't apply it to their golf swing, they aim right down the middle. If you aim down the middle, this would leave you with only half the fairway to catch your mistake. Using an inside-out swing path, you know your ball is going to fly a little bit left, so you can aim a little right and increase your landing area by 100 percent.

Aiming down the middle and not having a consistent swing path means your ball could go left or right, which equals no control. Learn a consistent inside-out swing path, as this is the first step to becoming a better player. Once your swing path repeats the same from swing to swing, having the clubface strike the ball correctly becomes a result of good timing, which will come to you through practice.

I once asked Masters champion Gay Brewer how many pros on the tour swing from the inside to the outside. "They all had better do it," said Gay. I also asked Steve Elkington, a great player and exceptional swinger of the golf club, if he thought it was a good idea to teach students to first draw the ball. His answer was, "Yes, that's how I would approach teaching."

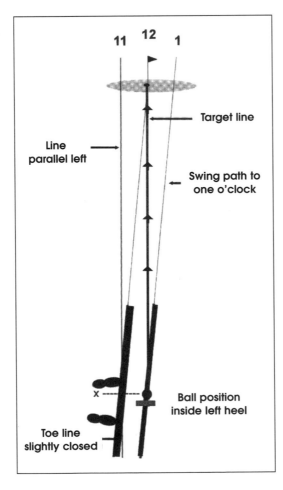

Figure 1.4 Alignment for the draw shot. The inside-out swing path gives both distance and control.

Establishing the Inside-Out Swing Path

Now I'm going to begin to show you how to establish an inside-out swing path, which is the first basic component to being able to draw the ball. Take a moment to look at Figure 1.4, which diagrams the alignment for a draw shot.

First lay a golf club down with the shaft pointing toward your target—this is your *toe line*. Now bring your toes up to the club shaft. Stand with your feet about shoulder width apart, the outside of your feet even with the outside of your shoulders. Your toes are now in line to your target. It's easier to swing from inside-out if you move your right foot slightly back from the line (half an inch is enough). You'll now notice that your toe line favors slightly to the right of target (you now have a bit of a closed stance, also known as the power stance). This stance does two important things for you. First, it makes it easier for you to swing back on an inside path. Also, in this stance your left shoulder is also favoring slightly right of target. Your toe line, hip line, and shoulder line are positioned equally. As you swing back, your left shoulder does not have as far to travel to get even with the ball, and this makes it easier for you to achieve a full backswing coil or turn.

While there, keep your knees relaxed and bend forward from the waist. Bend forward enough so that your arms hang straight down from your shoulders in a relaxed manner. Let your hands hang in front of you as if you are going to touch your toes. As a general rule, bend forward so your spine is tilted near 20 degrees forward, and your arms hang straight down comfortably. While in this forward leaning position, which I call golf's posture, your left hand (for right-handed golfers) will be close to being only a fist from your left thigh.

From this position, put your right hand on the side of your right leg and work solely with your left hand and arm. As you lean forward, we can call your head and spine the axis. Your upper body, during the swing, coils around that axis, but you don't want it going up and down. It is a fixed axis. I call the left shoulder your swing point. This is where the swing comes from. You can swing your glove hand and arm freely back and forth from that point.

Imagine your swing taking place on a vertical clock face (see Figure 1.5). During this exercise, just swing your glove hand and arm from seven o'clock through to five o'clock on the clock face. This is the impact area. It is when your glove hand comes to the bottom part of your swing.

Swinging your left arm from the shoulder in this way, take your glove hand back toward your right thigh, and as you keep it there, look and see how close it is. Then swing it through the impact area

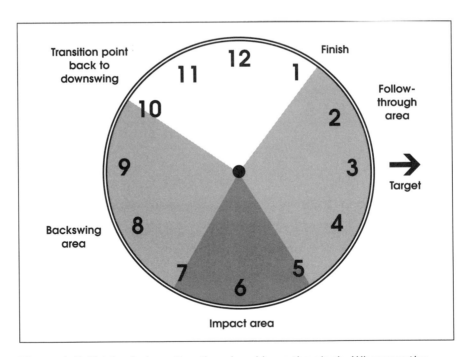

Figure 1.5 Think of where the glove hand is on the clock. Wherever the back of the glove hand goes, so goes the clubface.

and see that it is now opposite your left thigh and is a bit farther away than it was from your right thigh. You have just practiced an inside-out swing path. Your glove hand swings back on an inside path and follows that same path as it returns to the ball.

While doing this drill, keep your lower body still, keep your hips from moving out or turning, and keep the lower body quiet. You will notice as you swing your glove hand back and forth along this path that the path is not straight at your target, but a slight diagonal line through the ball. This is the only swing path that puts the type of spin on the ball that makes it fly farther.

As you perform this swing path, the back of your glove hand becomes your guide, your central control. So put your thinking in the back of your glove hand. Wherever the back of your glove hand goes, so goes your clubface. Think of the clubface as an extension of the back of the glove hand. As a golfer, you don't have to think way down where the golf ball is or where the clubhead is. You only have to think about what you are doing with the back of the glove hand as you swing it from your left shoulder. You can also think of having two clubfaces. One is the back of your glove hand and the other is the clubhead's clubface. Remember, put your thinking in the back of your glove hand.

11

As you swing your glove hand along the swing path and into and through the impact area, the speed will want to pull your head with it. The secret to the golf swing is to keep your head and left shoulder still while you are swinging your glove hand through impact. If you can do that, you'll be a good golfer.

Developing the Motor of the Swing

The following one-arm exercise will help you to develop left side control and muscle memory. This exercise also teaches the left side to be the leader, thus eliminating left side/right side muscle conflict that will rob you of swing smoothness and clubhead speed. We do it with the left arm and we do it for two reasons.

It will help you to get the golf club into the proper position at the top of the backswing. The backswing is the setup to the whole swing. If you are not right at the top of the backswing, your swing doesn't have much of a chance. Also, the backswing is like aiming a gun. If you take your time, you are more likely to hit your target. I'm not interested in speed into the backswing; you can take three weeks to get there. Go slow and get set into the proper position. The slower you go, the more feel you have. As Bobby Jones once said, "I never saw anyone go too slow."

The second thing this exercise is going to do is get you into the proper position, using the correct muscles—the left side muscles. The more you exercise the correct muscles, the stronger they get. The stronger they get, the more they remember. The more they remember, the less you have to think. This is muscle memory. An example of muscle memory is tying your shoes. You don't think about it, you just do it. Swinging the golf club is as easy as tying your shoes, provided that you use the same muscles and go to the same correct positions every time.

One-Arm Exercise Drill

During this exercise, stand on a driving range practice mat and focus on a two-inch rubber tee. Use a 7-iron. Stand in good golf posture with only your glove hand attached, with the clubhead positioned just behind the tee and facing the target. When you start back, it is very important what direction the club starts back from the tee (which represents the ball). You don't want to push your glove hand outside of the tee, away from your body, or straight back, but you do want to push your glove hand back on an inside track. This causes the clubhead to go back on an inside track, which is important to being able to hit a draw (which puts a spin on the ball that allows it to fly and roll farther).

Think of a golf swing as a pendulum. A pendulum swings back and up on one track and returns on the same track. This is what your glove hand does, so it is important how you take your glove hand back away from the ball, because you want it to return on the same track. As you push back, use your left side muscles, and push back and up to a point where your left arm is parallel to the ground, and hinge your wrist to create a 90-degree angle between your forearm and the club shaft. (At this time when you swing back having the left arm parallel to the ground is high enough. Later, in Chapter 3, we will complete the full backswing.)

I call this 90-degree angle *leverage*. It is your source of power. The farther you are from the 90-degree angle, the more open your swing is and the less power you will have. Once again, here is the exercise. Swinging from your left shoulder and using your left side muscles, swing your glove hand back on an inside path and up to a spot where your left arm is parallel to the ground and you have your 90-degree wrist hinge.

Stand with your feet about shoulder width apart, which is the outside of your feet even with the outside of your shoulders. (As far as ball position is concerned, we will play the ball off of the inside of the left heel. I recommend that until you become a fairly good player, you play that same ball position with all of your clubs. It makes things simpler for you, you'll get used to seeing it there and get comfortable with it there, and having the ball in the same spot will help your timing.) Now put your glove hand (left hand for a right-handed player) on the club. After positioning the glove hand on the club and before going into the backswing, hold the club up in front of you so the left arm and club shaft are parallel to the ground. As you hold it there, I will show you three checkpoints that you want to look at and be aware of each time before you swing the club:

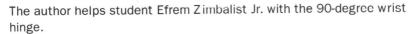
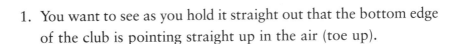

The author helps student Efrem Zimbalist Jr. with the 90-degree wrist hinge.

1. You want to see as you hold it straight out that the bottom edge of the club is pointing straight up in the air (toe up).

2. The "V" formed by your thumb and index finger should point between your neck and your right shoulder. This is referred to as a neutral grip. It is the position used by most of the best golfers. The neutral grip is the grip that I teach.

3. The third checkpoint is to have the bottom pad of your glove hand on top of the grip. This position tells you that the grip of the club is settled properly in your hand. As you hold it like this, you should be able to lift your thumb off, along with the first three fingers. Now you are holding it with just the bottom pad of your hand and your little finger. This is helpful because your little finger is one of the major grippers of the left hand and it needs to be able to clamp around the grip. (Grip is discussed in detail in Chapter 4.)

Before you make each swing, it is important that you have the same glove hand/clubhead relationship. This is the first step in developing consistent feel of clubhead position, and a must ingredient for good timing and grip security.

First Move: The Backswing

Now, using only the glove hand and arm, take the club back and up to the top of the backswing. As you take it up, keep your face square to the ground and your eyes on the tee (keep the head still). Once your glove is at the top, look for these three checkpoints:

1. Left arm parallel to the ground, glove hand even with toe line.

2. Ninety-degree angle between the left forearm and the shaft of the club.

3. Notice also that the back of the glove hand is laid back near 20 degrees. This lays the shaft back 20 degrees. The angle of the shaft is referred to as your *swing plane*. The back of your glove hand controls the angle of the shaft, so the back of your glove hand controls the swing plane.

15

Let's go one more time into the backswing from the start. From your left shoulder, swing your glove hand back on an inside path and up to a point where your left arm is parallel to the ground and your glove hand is even with your toe line. You've got a 90-degree angle between the club shaft and your forearm, and your glove hand is laid back near 20 degrees. This is the first step to being in the proper position at the top of the backswing. Both swings have used the same muscles to go to the same place. This is the beginning to your golf swing having the ability to repeat itself.

Try this experiment: take your glove hand and put it halfway into your pocket. Do it again. Take it out and put it there a third time. As

The author with PGA Senior Tour player "Mr. 59," Al Geiberger, demonstrating the 20-degree swing plane angle.

you do that, you'll notice that your pocket does not move—it's always in the same place. Here is your thought as a golfer: you want to swing your glove hand up into an imaginary pocket at the top of your backswing. Like the pocket of your pants, this pocket should always be in the same place. You use the same muscles to swing into the same imaginary pocket at the top of the backswing every time.

Though I'm not there with you, I can tell you that each time you put your glove hand into your pants pocket, you went into the pocket at the same angle. This is what you want to do as you swing up into the imaginary pocket at the top of the backswing. You want your glove hand to swing to the same pocket, and you want it to be the same angle laid back 20 degrees every time. Same pocket, same angle. Now you will always swing your glove hand down and through the ball from the same stop point at the top of the backswing. This is the

Senior PGA Tour Star Miller Barber on Repeatability

Miller Barber had this to say: "If someone would say to me he could repeat his effective swing more than anyone else, that's what I'd like to hear. That is what this is all about and it is what I've tried to do all these years."

first step toward being more aware of where your body parts are, and being able to feel the same backswing position each time.

The Downswing

At the top of the backswing, keep your head and left shoulder still. (Your left shoulder has coiled back and is now over the ball or slightly behind the ball.) Swing your glove hand down from your left shoulder. Don't drop or move your shoulder toward your target, just swing your glove hand straight down from it as if gravity were bringing it down. You control it coming down, but your thought is that you bring it down as if gravity were bringing it down.

The result is that as your glove hand comes down, the angles don't change, you keep your 90-degree power angle and you keep your 20-degree laid back swing plane angle. (In Chapter 3 we will discuss this action in more detail.)

Through-Swing to Finish

Now I want to walk you through impact and up to the finish. With a 7-iron in hand, position your body as if you were addressing the ball. When you are in a good position, place your right hand on the side of your right leg. As you hold on to the club with your glove hand, swing your left arm from your left shoulder on an inside-out path. As the clubhead swings through the tee, it makes a noise. This is impact. After swinging your glove hand through the impact area a couple of times, swing through the impact area and rotate your glove hand through it. This sets the left arm (wrist and elbow) in position to go up into the finish without strain in these areas. As you go up into the finish, do not look, but feel your way. Once you are in the finish, rotate your head to take a look, but do not pick up your head. With the glove hand in the finish position, look for these checkpoints:

1. The butt of the club is pointing at the target like a barrel on a gun.

2. The club shaft is behind you, parallel to the ground like a clothesline.

3. The upper part of the arm (the biceps/triceps area) is parallel to the ground.

4. The glove hand is even with your toe line.

5. These things combine to form a box effect between your left arm and the club shaft.

At this point, as your glove hand and arm go into the finish position, maintain your golf posture (the forward tilt of the upper body at a near 20-degree spine angle). Make sure your chin is not too low, as you don't want it too close to the chest. Your head should be up enough so that the chin doesn't cause the shoulder coil to take your head out of position. New players tend to have their chin too low. If you wear bifocal glasses, this may cause you to put your chin too low because you are trying to get a clear view over the top of the split screen. This head position restricts the shoulder coil and can take the head out of its ideal balance position. If you wear bifocals and are really interested in swinging better, I suggest you take your glasses off during lessons and see if you can get another pair of glasses without bifocal lenses.

Once again practice swinging your glove hand through impact and up into the finish, keeping your head still until the glove hand has landed in the finish position. It is important to always keep the head still until the swing has come to a stop. Then rotate your head and take a look at where the glove hand finished, and you should see the exact same position you saw before. The glove hand is now into another imaginary pocket, this time in the finish position. We are already beginning to build repetition into your muscle motion.

Now go to the top of the backswing again, and remember that your glove hand should be even with the toe line. From there bring your glove hand down, through, and up into the finish position and see that on the finish side, the glove hand is again even with the toe line. Notice that your glove hand is even with your toe line on both sides of the swing.

Observe what happens with the toe of the club as you go through impact and up into the finish. Earlier I talked of rotating your glove hand through impact enough to set your wrist and elbow hinges in a position that allows you to swing up into the finish with no pressure

Tip to Keep the Chin Up

For golfers who tend to have their chin and head too low, here's a tip to keep the chin up: look at the ball as if you are looking at it through your nostrils. Granted this could be a hairy view if you really could look through, but it does keep the chin from getting too close to the chest.

in these areas, no strain. Well, you also want to rotate enough so as you go up into the finish, the toe of the club is straight up. From this position it is ready to go up into the finish very fast and clean. If you over-rotate, however, and the toe of the club is pointing left of your target, it acts like an airplane wing. It will pull your club too far left, resulting in a big hook, your ball going too far left. If you don't rotate enough and the toe of your club is pointing right of your target, the clubface is then open and you are asking the ball to escape to the right, resulting in a big slice.

This glove hand and forearm rotation through the ball is a very important part of a good golf swing. The timing of the rotation plus your swing path combine to allow you to control the spin on the ball. The pros refer to the clubhead of an iron as the *blade*, and they describe this rotation as *working the blade through the ball*.

20

The Quarter Turn

I have a term for this glove hand rotation through the ball, which was first published in an article I wrote for *Golf Tips* magazine in 1991. I call this glove hand rotation the *quarter turn*, and I'll tell you why. Put your glove hand on the golf club in the proper position and hold the club straight out in front of you so that your left arm and the club shaft are parallel to the ground. Now look at the clubhead. You should see that the toe of the club is straight up in the air, and so is the bottom edge of your club (I use a 7-iron while teaching). Now use your glove hand and forearm and rotate the toe of the club 90 degrees to the left, then return it to the upright position. You just did a hand and forearm rotation of 90 degrees, or a quarter turn. (Notice this is a hand and forearm rotation, not a wrist hinge.) Now hold the club up again with the toe straight up. From there rotate the toe of the club 90 degrees to the right. Keep it there a moment, then rotate the toe and the club all the way around so the toe is now pointing left: you have just done a 180-degree rotation with your glove hand and clubhead. This full 180-degree rotation occurs through impact, but from impact up into the finish you want only 90 degrees of rotation.

When you get really good at this through practice, you will hit more greens and more fairways. Keep in mind that this is a precision timing movement, and practice for only 90 degrees or a quarter turn with your glove hand and forearm. Here we are talking about what happens through impact, which is the most sensitive part of the swing. This action is not that difficult. I teach people from all walks of life, men and women ages five to ninety-five, people with different skill levels, coordination levels, and IQs, and everybody gets it, so I'm not worried about you.

Demonstration of Left Side Control

Here is a demonstration of left side control I use with my students. I ask the student to stand about twelve feet away from me and be my

Margin of Error

Golfers have a margin of error through impact. If you're a little late with the rotation or a little too aggressive, you still have an opportunity to catch a part of the fairway or green. When you have perfect rotation timing, the ball flies to your target as if it's on a string. Here is the good news—golf club manufacturers are constantly striving to improve the performance of clubs to help the golfer return the clubface squarely behind the ball at the moment of impact.

Tournament Player Advice

LPGA Hall of Fame player Patty Berg: "You cannot get away without having the proper fundamentals. Little flaws in your swing become big flaws when the pressure is on. Top players strive for perfection and always practice to conquer the little flaws."

Tour player Greg Norman: "Eighty percent of all golfers are slicers."

Two-time Senior British Open champion Brian Barnes of Scotland: "My left side controls my swing."

target. Using only the one-arm exercise, I swing back, down, and through to the finish. I hold the finish and point out that the butt of the club is pointing at the target like the barrel of a gun, and my glove hand is even with my toe line. I then ask the student to watch again, and this time I shadow the action with my right hand. As I hold the finish, I point out that the glove hand is in the same position. Next I attach the right hand, but tell the student that when I finish, he or she will see the same glove hand position because the right side is only going for the ride. I swing back, down, through, and up to the finish again, and the student sees both hands on the club in a finished position. Once again, I point out that the glove hand is in the same position, because it has been well educated and well rehearsed. It knows where it's going in relationship to the target. I swing once more with both hands on and full leg action, and the student sees the same exact glove hand position at the finish.

The point of this demonstration is that when you see a top player swing a club, he or she is not just swinging all over the place. The player is well aware of what is going on with the glove hand. Think of your glove hand as being on a flight. It is flying from point A, the top of the backswing, to point B, the finish. You've got to know where point A is and where point B is and what happens between those two points. What happens is your glove hand picks up the swing path, does the rotation through impact, and you do it all with a still head.

That concludes my first lesson. When I give this first lesson in a live situation it takes about thirty minutes. Now that you have an overview of the inside-out swing, in the following chapters we will build your swing piece by piece.

2

THROUGH-SWING: IMPACT THROUGH FINISH

K now the destination before you start the journey. Think of a golf swing as a complete circle. The follow-through to the finish is half the circle. The backswing and downswing is the other half. The two sides are equally important.

Glove Hand Grip Review

As you hold your club straight out in front of you, the toe of the club and the bottom edge point straight up in the air. The "V" formed by your thumb and index finger points between your neck and your right shoulder. The bottom pad of the glove hand is on top of the grip.

Rehearsing the Finish

What happens from impact up into the finish takes a split second to occur. When your clubhead enters the impact area and comes in contact with the ball at 100 m.p.h., the ball is on the clubface for less than one-hundredth of a second. In a complete round of golf, the ball will be on the clubface for a total of less than half a second. In a four-day tournament, the ball will be on the clubface only around two seconds.

My teaching method has proven that all people are able to control their finish. As you follow the framework of a fundamentally sound swing by first walking your way through in slow motion, you become more aware of the feel of what is correct. Through exercising and rehearsing your swing this takes on the guise of being automatic, but it is not. You must stay focused throughout every repetition by visualizing the swing and using thought control. This is sometimes called *feel*. You know the feel through practice. But you can only repeat good feel through concentration and focus.

For this lesson, take your 7-iron out of your bag, put your glove on, and take your stance to the target. We are continuing to teach the left side to be the leader. The details of the follow-through to finish are as important as the details of the backswing.

While we work on going up into the finish, try to maintain the forward tilt of your upper body. Bend at the waist so your spine angle is near 20 degrees and your arms hang comfortably straight down from your shoulders. As you swing into the finish work on not lifting the upper body. Swing your glove hand up but not your body.

Now I'm ready to guide you up into the finish. Remember that in the last lesson I asked you to finish with the butt of the club toward the target, like the barrel of a gun. I pointed out that at the finish your glove hand is even with your toe line and the golf club shaft is parallel to the ground. You have formed a box effect between your left arm and the golf club shaft. Remember that as your glove hand followed the swing path it rotated a quarter turn to set your left elbow and left wrist in position to go up to the finish with no stress on the

PGA Tour player Tom
Purtzer maintaining
spine angle through
impact.

27

joints. The quarter turn of the glove hand through impact also
resulted in the toe of the club being straight up in the air as you
swung into the finish.

The Glass Wall

As you stand in your start position (in golf terms we call this your
address position), your toe line is your target line. Imagine a glass
wall eight feet tall extending from your left toe toward your target.
As you swing your glove hand through impact, rotate it so that the
back of your glove hand can now slide up on this glass wall. As you
hold your finish and look at your glove hand position you now see and

The left hand/left arm box effect at finish.

feel the same thing as before, but now you know there is a glass wall. Why the glass wall? If at the moment of impact the clubface was a little closed, it would act like an airplane wing, pulling your clubhead left, breaking the glass wall and causing a big hook to the left. If your clubface was a little open at impact and you broke the glass wall, that would spin the ball off to the right, resulting in a big slice. By not breaking the glass wall you'll eliminate the big mistakes.

We now start to focus in on the target as we swing into the finish. This is where a baseball swing and a golf swing depart company. A baseball flies chest high so you swing around, but a golf ball is on the ground so you swing down through and more upright. A baseball swing is horizontal to the ground, but a golf swing is more vertical. Pro golfers that you could look at and study as they swing up into the

The glass wall as illustrated in *Golf Tips* magazine, October 1998. Used by permission.

finish are Greg Norman, Jack Nicklaus, Hale Irwin, and Tom Purtzer (voted best swing on tour by his fellow players). Those swings fall within the framework of the pure, classic, target-oriented golf swing we are talking about here. The key here is that you rotate your glove enough through impact that as you go up into the finish the back of the glove hand is in position to slide up the glass wall. This is essential for you to quickly become a better ball striker.

Pull Toward One O'Clock in the Field

Let's go up into the finish another time, but before we do, keep thinking that your toe line is your target line. I want you to think of a big clock lying in the field, and think of your target as twelve o'clock.

Kermit Zarley on the Glass Wall Swing

Senior PGA Tour player Kermit Zarley (on Tour since 1963) discussed the glass wall swing with me:

Kermit: As I swing into the finish, I try to make sure that I keep the club going up on the target line as I'm coming into my upswing so that by the time I finish my swing, I don't get my shaft too much across the target line. I want to swing more down the line, like Nicklaus always was. It's a more upright swing plane. I don't want to swing around my body like in baseball.

Glenn: Would the thought be, let's say you are my target and between you and me I put a glass wall here, and I want to slide the back of my glove hand up on the glass wall rather than breaking the glass wall. Is that a good thought?

Kermit: Exactly. I try to swing the club back down and up visualizing that plane.

When we spoke of the swing path we talked of an inside-out path, a slight diagonal through the ball—think now of that path leading a bit to the right of your target—let's call that one o'clock. This time as you swing your glove hand through the impact area and rotate through, make sure that you pull your glove hand toward one o'clock and up as you go into the finish. If you pull your glove hand toward twelve o'clock, your target, you will break the glass wall, and you open up a can of worms for bad shots. As you hold your finish after swinging toward one o'clock, you see and feel the same position as before. But now you know that there is a glass wall and that you are swinging your glove hand toward one o'clock and up on one o'clock. (See Figure 1.3 in Chapter 1.)

Now I'll guide you up into the finish again. This time do the same action, while following an inside-out swing path and doing a glove hand and forearm rotation through impact. Go through the bottom of the swing toward one o'clock in the field and up on one o'clock. Make sure you rotate through impact enough so you are in position for the back of the glove to slide up on the glass wall. In the finish position you'll notice the butt of the club is pointing toward your target, your glove hand is even with your toe line, the club shaft is behind you like a clothesline, and you have the same left arm box effect as before.

End in the Waiter Position

Keep your glove hand in the finish position, but take the club out of it with your other hand and open the glove hand fully. You should appear almost like a waiter holding a tray. At this moment you don't want to have your palm flat looking to the sky, nor do you want your fingers to point to the sky. What you want is your hand laid back near 40 degrees or almost like a waiter.

There are two main reasons for this waiter position. Remember that a golf swing takes about 1.3 seconds, and we are talking about what takes place within that time frame. We are talking about tenths and hundredths of a second. Consider this: by the time a pro's glove hand goes into the backswing and returns to the ball, he wants that to be a second or more. You can see that all of the real speed is through impact and up into the finish. The finish side of the swing only takes half a second or less. Here is my point—if you can land your glove hand in the finish position that I am mapping out for you, then you pretty much had to be in the proper position at impact. Being able to land your glove hand in this position gives you insurance that you were pretty close to being where you should have been at the moment of impact.

The glove hand should finish laid back near 40 degrees, almost like a waiter carrying a tray.

If someone were to ask me what I thought the most important part of the golf swing was, I'd say a still head. "[The] head still is the absolute fundamental," said Jack Nicklaus. As a teacher I take a still head and build a golf swing around it, the final result being that you end up having the absolute fundamental. The purpose for detailing out the finish position as we are doing is this: If you understood and can duplicate where your glove hand lands in the finish in relationship to where the target is, then you are better able to have a still head.

Each time you bring your glove hand up into the finish, concentrate as to where it lands. Develop a mental image of where your glove hand lands and then always try to land in the same spot. Swinging with precision, with a fundamentally sound golf swing, will enable timing to come to your swing faster.

Using the Finish to Detect Flaws

Most flaws that are visible in the finish can be traced backward to a point where the flaw began earlier. If you are not in the correct position at the finish, then chances are you were not in the correct position at impact.

The Finish Position

As I demonstrate the finish position, there are two things that help you to have a still head as you swing up to the top. First, make sure you don't break the glass wall. If your glove hand swings too far left of your target, it will pull your head along with it. When the head gets out of position, it causes bad shots. If you break the glass wall and your clubface is a little too closed at impact, you get a hook. If you break the glass wall with your glove hand and your clubface is a little open, you cut across the ball and ask it to escape to the right. Swinging toward one o'clock and sliding the back of your glove hand up the glass wall helps keep the head still.

Finish with the butt of the club toward the target like a barrel on a gun and have your glove hand in the waiter position. Create a box effect with your left arm from the shoulder to the elbow, parallel to the ground. Swinging higher than this position would pick up your head, which could cause a bladed or topped shot. On each swing concentrate on where you are landing your glove hand in relation to your target. Practice swinging up to the top with only your left hand and arm. When you do attach the right arm later, let it go for the ride.

33

Balance as You Hold Your Finish

Balance is the key to becoming a better golfer, faster. Two major factors can help you have a more solidly balanced finish: keeping your head still and maintaining balance.

No matter where you are in the golf swing, your upper body weight should stay between your feet. That is how it is when you stand, walk, and run, and that is how it is when good players swing a golf club. Keeping your head still keeps your upper body weight distributed evenly between your feet, and you are then more likely to have good balance.

You have seen a high-wire walker at the circus; he's got that long pole to help him balance. Think of your golf club as a balancing instrument. As you hold your finish, the shaft is parallel to the ground and the weight of the club is on one end and your glove hand is on the other. Hold on with your glove hand and use that golf club to help you balance. This also has the following two good side effects.

Use your golf club as a balancing tool like a circus high-wire walker's pole, keeping constant grip pressure all the way up to the finish.

Why I Teach the Finish in the Second Lesson

The reason I teach the finish in the second lesson is simply that if you know how to swing through impact and up into the finish first, when you build the backswing and downswing to impact you will already know what to do from there. Think of a golf swing as a journey: you know the destination before you start the trip. When you can visualize the finish you know what muscles you're using and what path you're following. Then through repetition you will establish an awareness of where your body parts are in space and time. As a result you will develop a better feel for the fundamentally sound positions and a feel for the smooth, effortless physical swinging of the club. A big key to this end is to know the destination before you start the journey.

One reason unschooled golfers have a bad shot is that they don't finish their swing. By knowing how and where to finish in relationship to your target, you will now always make a full finish and eliminate a reason for a bad shot.

Another reason unschooled golfers make bad shots is their grip pressure changes somewhere during their swing. By holding on with the glove hand and using the golf club as a balancing instrument, you keep constant grip pressure all the way up to the finish, eliminating another reason for a bad shot. The more reasons for bad shots you can eliminate, the more good shots you will have.

Think of a golf swing as a complete circle, and your head as the center of the circle. When you make impact, you are in the middle of a swing. This is no time to sightsee, so a good rule, especially when you are working toward being a better ball striker, is to keep your head still until your glove hand lands in the finish, until the swing is finished and you are holding your finish. Strive for solid balance at the finish.

THE FINISH IN REVIEW

1. Glove hand follows inside-out path and does a quarter turn through impact (a glove hand/forearm 90-degree rotation).

2. Glove swings out toward one o'clock in the field and up on one o'clock.

3. Back of glove slides up on the glass wall.

4. Glove hand ends in a position that it is almost like a waiter, lying back near 40 degrees when fingers open fully.

5. The golf club is used as a balancing pole.

After completing your swing, hold your finish position and use the following checkpoints to evaluate the swing.

36

YOUR FINISH CHECKPOINTS

1. The butt of the club is toward the target like a barrel of a gun. (Playing golf is one big target shoot.)

2. Glove hand is even with your toe line.

3. Golf club shaft is behind you like a clothesline, horizontal to the ground.

4. Your upper body did not lift. You favor your weight on the left foot as you hold your finish.

5. When you finally look to see the ball fly, even then don't pick your head up, but just rotate it—keep your head weight in position even when you take a look. Each time you practice going into the finish, hold the finish. When it is time to look at where you are, rotate your head to take a look, but do not pick up your head. Let your head stay in position until the golf swing has come to a good balanced finish and all body parts are quiet.

Two Clocks

I don't want to confuse you, but now we have two clocks. One is lying flat in the field (as in Figures 1.3 and 1.4), your target being twelve o'clock. The other is vertical, and you are standing in it as I look at you. (This clock was introduced in Figure 1.5 in Chapter 1.)

Hinge at Four O'Clock

The proper positioning of the left arm as you pull it through and up into the finish is a very important action of your swing. Knowing when and how to hinge your elbow and wrist as you go into the finish will do these three things for you.

1. Eliminate stress in those areas

2. Increase clubhead speed

3. Help the clubhead consistently return to the ball with the loft intended depending on the club in your hand

37

The proper sequence of hinging will increase your percentage of good shots.

As you rotate your glove through impact and are pulling toward one o'clock in the field, you have rotated enough to set your hinges in a position that allows you to go up into the finish smoothly and easily. You've also rotated enough so the back of your glove hand is ready to slide up the glass wall and the toe of the club is straight up. Now the club is in position to go up fast and smooth. As you are in this position, you can also use your biceps muscle to take you up from there.

Even though I'm asking you to use the biceps muscle, you don't want to "muscle" the action. When you walk you use muscles, but you don't "muscle" yourself down a sidewalk. Swimmers use muscles, but they don't muscle themselves through the water. Similarly, in golf as you swing up into the finish you should be in a position to use this muscle without muscling the action.

By using your biceps in a comfortable manner, you can direct the swing up, rather than around your body. To put a draw spin on the ball, you want to swing up into the target, not across your target. The use of the biceps causes the elbow to hinge. Let's pinpoint the moment that we want the elbow to hinge.

Think of yourself as being in a clock. As you pull through with your left side, pick up the swing path and rotate through the ball, which is at six o'clock, as your glove goes through to five o'clock and on to four o'clock. It is at this moment that you want your elbow to hinge. If you go up to three o'clock and you haven't hinged yet, it's too late. You've topped the ball. The elbow hinge should begin at four o'clock. (See Figure 2.1.)

The elbow hinge should begin at the four o'clock position.

Here's why. Remember that your left side is the leader and the right side is the follower. I want you not to think of your right arm as an arm anymore but as a towel. If we measure it from your right shoulder to the fingertips, it is only so long. As your left side pulls your right side through impact and your glove hand reaches four o'clock, it is at this moment that your right arm has been pulled to a full extension. At this point one of two things has to happen.

1. If you don't hinge your left elbow at four o'clock, your head would be pulled up or toward the target, which could lead to other flaws.

2. By hinging at four o'clock you are now better able to maintain a still head—and having a still head is the absolute fundamental in a good golf swing.

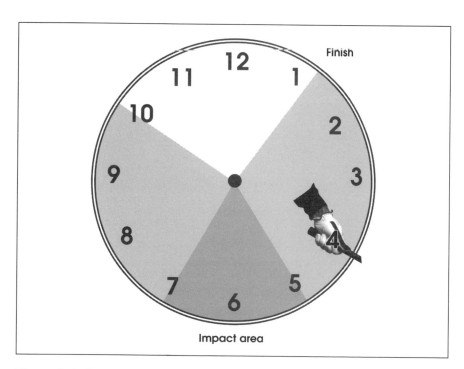

Figure 2.1 Glove hand at four o'clock, the point in the swing where the elbow hinge should begin.

Now consider a one-arm swing with the left arm through impact and up into the finish. You already know that the elbow hinges at four o'clock, but at what point does the wrist hinge? The answer is that the wrist hinges *after* the elbow. This sequence will help you to become a more consistent ball striker.

In the action of unschooled golfers, the sequence of hinging is reversed. The wrist hinges before the elbow. This is because they haven't been taught that the left side is the leader and the right side is the follower. Most people are right-handed, and the right side has a God-given, automatic impulse to get involved. In most cases the problem this creates is that it pushes through impact, and the wrist then hinges before the elbow.

There are at least five errors that result from that single flaw:

1. The right side push creates a scooping effect with the clubface, like scooping ice cream. This changes the loft of the club. If you have a 36-degree 7-iron and you push through, you could change the loft to anywhere from 36 to 56 degrees depending on the amount that the right side is involved. Many players come to me and say, "I'm not getting consistent distance with my irons." As soon as they say that I know their right hand or arm is pushing, causing the wrist to hinge before the elbow. This results in the clubface nearing impact with different loft from swing to swing.

2. A low screamer, the bladed shot. Here the right hand pushes the bottom edge of the blade into the center of the ball.

3. The topped shot (the weak, very short shot)—your right hand gets way too active and pushes the bottom edge of the blade into the top of the ball.

4. The whiff—you miss the ball completely. The right hand has pushed so much that the wrist is hinged way before impact and the bottom edge of the club is pushed clean over the ball.

5. The fifth mistake that occurs as a result of the wrist hinging before the elbow is the fat shot—this occurs when the wrist hinges way too early, as you are swinging down into the ball. Here your wrist hinges at about nine o'clock because you got really anxious to hit the ball. This causes your clubhead speed to be thrown too soon, which drops the upper body, and you hit the ground first. That's the fat shot. Your body motion would resemble someone chopping wood. When the body drops your swing goes down, and you lose a level swing.

Those five errors can be eliminated by pulling through impact with your left side and hinging the elbow before the wrist as you follow through into the finish. When this is done correctly, your clubhead stays low through the impact area.

The thought is that you want to sweep your club through the ball. This can be called a *pull sweep* because you are pulling through with your left side. Don't forget to rotate through impact. As you go through impact you pull sweep and rotate your left glove hand and forearm.

41

If you are using a 7-iron with 36 degrees of loft correctly, your pull sweep will always pull 36 degrees into the ball, every time. This is a big key to getting consistent distance with your irons.

Follow-Through to Finish: The Key to Speed

When you swing correctly into the finish, you will have an effortless feeling. The follow-through and finish of the swing is where your clubhead flies the fastest. Keep in mind that a golf swing takes about one and a half seconds for the whole action to complete. From the time your glove hand starts back into the backswing and returns to the ball, the pro wants that to be a second or more. So that leaves only a half a second from impact up into the finish. You've got to get yourself into position, and you've got to be ready to accommodate all that speed.

Five things occur as you swing through the ball up into the finish:

1. You rotate your glove hand enough so your elbow and wrist are in position to hinge, without stress or pressure in those areas.

2. You've done a quarter turn through impact, and now the toe of the club is straight up in the air. This is its most aerodynamic position. It is ready to fly fast and clean.

3. You have rotated enough so that the back of your glove hand is in position to slide up the glass wall.

4. As you go up into the finish you are in a position where you could use your biceps muscle.

5. Rotation through impact creates clubhead torque. It's like the afterburner of the jet—the clubhead accelerates.

All five of those things add up to you being able to swing faster into the finish.

Impact Through Finish One-Arm Drill

I am getting you ready to go very fast. As you walk yourself through the ball and into the finish, do this many times with the glove hand and arm only. (Figure 2.2 shows glove hand position through impact and up into the finish.) Swing from the shoulder, and as your glove hand swings through impact up into the finish, try not to let your head go forward. Keep your head between your feet and keep the lower body quiet for now. We will add the leg action later. At this stage of your development, while you hold your finish, it is okay to slightly favor your hip weight over your left shoelaces. Be on top of the shoe or a little on the inside edge, but not outside of the shoe.

How far back should you go, and how many times should you do this one-arm swing? Only swing back to seven o'clock, and then pull through impact and up into the finish.

Repetitions equal certainty; do however many it takes for you to teach the left side to be the leader, to strengthen the left side, to be familiar with the feel of left side control, to get to a level of comfort for the exercise, and finally to get muscle memory. When I teach, I physically guide the student each time, working on the same muscles, going to the same positions. I usually recommend fifteen hours of instruction. Proper repetitions have a positive result, the student following the same pattern each time. In the same way, you can check

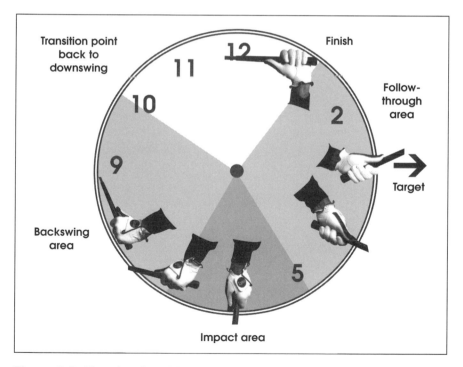

Figure 2.2 Glove hand position through impact and up into the finish.

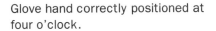

Glove hand correctly positioned at four o'clock.

Glove hand position at finish, with the butt of the club toward the target.

your position with each swing to make sure you are practicing the correct movements.

Once the left side has been taught to pull through and be the leader, then I add the right hand and arm to the club. This is the subject of Chapter 4. For now, think of the right arm as a towel that the left arm is going to pull through. Offer no resistance with the right, keep it relaxed. Let it go with the flow. You want no use or effort coming from the right side. Adding the right side to this drill is described in Chapter 4.

To Ensure a Still Head, Hit Against a Brick Wall

As you are standing over the ball in your start position, think of a wall going from your left eye down to the inside of your left foot.

The author at address
position, showing the brick
wall image to keep the head
and lower body still.

Your head is the top of the wall and your left leg and foot are the bottom of the wall.

This wall is selective as to what can pass through it. Your glove hand can go through, but your head and lower body cannot. (This is akin to a term from biology you might know, *semipermeable membrane*.) If your head would move forward during impact, then the top of the wall moves and it is a weak hit.

If your lower body moves, the bottom of the wall moves and it is a weak hit. You want to create this wall so you have something solid to hit against at impact. Keeping the head still and the lower body still at impact allows the glove hand to put a strong hit on the ball. When the clubhead meets the ball, you are in the middle of your swing. Keep swinging your glove hand up to a complete finish.

The Full Finish

The trademark statement of all well-schooled players is a complete balanced finish. A full finished swing helps speed, accuracy, and balance. As you swing up to the finish, don't stop until you reach the top.

In the next lesson we will talk about the backswing, downswing, and through impact action. It has always been my approach in teaching golf that you build a golf swing from the waist up, adding leg action last. While we are going through this and the next lesson, keep in mind a good general weight rule. Allow your weight to follow your glove hand, because the glove hand leads the action. Until we talk details about the legs, only feel a slight change in weight as you swing back and through.

46

The author and Efrem Zimbalist Jr. demonstrate a complete balanced finish.

Understand and practice each lesson before you move on to the next one. Build your golf swing one part at a time. Soon it will all come together and you'll follow the pattern of a fundamentally sound golf swing. When you have the time, watch and study the finishes of these three great players:

- **Jack Nicklaus:** He was voted best player of the century. His swing is an example of knowledge and physical action flowing in perfect harmony. To his credit he won seventy PGA tournaments.
- **Greg Norman:** Greg learned by watching Jack Nicklaus. He has won three Vardon Trophies, and his swing put him on top of the world in rankings for an unmatched ninety-six weeks in a row.
- **Hale Irwin:** His swing has been called majestic. He has won three U.S. Open championships and one Senior U.S. Open championship. He has set many Senior Tour records.

47

Tournament Player Advice

According to Colorado Hall of Fame golfer and Colorado Open champion Ted Hart, "The finish is like the last chapter of a novel, it tells the whole story."

3

BACKSWING, DOWNSWING, AND IMPACT: SWING PATH AND POWER ANGLE

You are the pilot flying your clubhead. Remember always, steady as she goes. In this lesson we continue to focus on the action of the glove hand (left hand for right-handed golfers). Remember to put your thinking in the back of your glove hand. We begin by using only the left arm, continuing to educate and build up the strength of the motor of the swing. The backswing is about extension, creating a full arc in balance—it is not about speed. A good general rule to follow is that the upper body coil causes the lower body coil. Reproducing the same sound backswing every time helps you to have the strongest motion into the ball.

The author with Efrem Zimbalist Jr., initiating the backswing.

50

Keep Your Right Side Relaxed

While I'm guiding you through each step of the backswing, try to keep your right side relaxed. Another way of saying that is to feel dead weight on the right side. Once we attach the right hand and you swing with both hands on, you still will want total relaxation from your right side. Right side tension is the culprit of many undesirable shots. As you follow along with me and walk through the swing using only your left side, there will be moments that you'll notice, even though your right side is not attached, that it will have a tendency to pull back, up, or show tension. When that occurs, take the time to relax it or shake it out. The first step to being able to relax the right side is to be aware of the presence of tension. Even after we put your swing together properly and you go out and practice, if you hit one million practice balls, on the next swing you will still have to remind yourself to relax your right side. It always wants to get involved. Through concentrating on relaxing it and practicing relaxing it you will find that your swing feels more coordinated, fast, and smooth. Your result will be more accuracy and more distance.

Post Weight and Begin Upper Body Coil

As we start this lesson, think of yourself back in the clock introduced in Chapter 1 (see Figure 1.5). Swing your glove hand on an inside track from your left shoulder ball-and-socket joint. Even though your spine angle represents the axis that your upper body coils around, the swing comes from your left shoulder, which I term the *swing point*. It is where the left hand and arm swing comes from.

When you start your glove hand back, for the first few inches, keep your lower body from moving. On the way back inside with your glove hand, it passes the crease of your right pant leg (mid thigh). This is when you post your weight on your right foot. You want to feel that your right hip weight is directly over the top of your right shoelaces.

Your right leg now becomes a post that you coil around as you continue into and up to the top of the backswing. Like a fence post it is perpendicular to the ground (straight up). Create the post early, keep the weight there, and coil around the post. Straight and comfortable are the key words for the right leg. Keep a slight flex in the right knee.

Follow with Lower Body Coil

Before we go further into what the left arm and hand do as they continue into the backswing, it is very important that you understand the lower body action of the backswing.

Reaching back with your glove hand starts or leads the coil. The upper body coil causes the lower body coil. Here is the sequence as you coil back.

1. Glove hand starts back on an inside path.

2. Left arm follows.

3. Left shoulder begins to go back with the flow. Your weight is now on your right side.

4. When your left shoulder touches your chin on the way back, allow your head to go slightly back with the flow.

5. Back coils with the reach.

6. Waist coils back.

7. Left hip coils back.

8. Left knee coils back.

This is the sequence, and it should be a slow, smooth sequence of events. As Senior PGA Tour player and long-ball hitter Dewitt Weaver says, "Backswing weight shift is a big power key. Try not to get weight outside of your right foot. What you want is balance over the right side so you can then move into the ball."

52

Golf Club Under Right Shoe Drill

Continuing to build the backswing, let's place the grip of a golf club under your right shoe. Place it under the outside edge of your shoe to keep the weight on the inside edge. When you swing up to the top of the backswing, you want to feel that your weight is a little on the inside of your right foot because from here you swing down and through toward your target. You have to set your body so it is ready to go to the target. Like a track star in the blocks, you are ready to burst out.

If your weight is on the outside of your right foot when you are at the top of your backswing, your lower body will never catch up as your glove hand swings down and through. This causes your swing to be out of sync. By having the weight a little on the inside of the right foot, you help the timing of the swing. The golf club under your shoe exaggerates this weight feel, but what you want to feel is 90 percent of your weight on top of your right shoe and 10 percent on the inside edge—but nothing outside. In a conversation I had with Mas-

The author with student Chuck Jackson demonstrating use of club under right shoe to keep weight on the inside of the right foot. The club lying in front of the toes points to the target. Your toe line is the target line.

53

ters champion Charles Coody, I said, "What if you have weight outside your right foot at the top of the backswing?" "Then your swing is dead. You've lost your power and timing," he answered.

While swinging into the backswing, the general rule for the lower body will always be *less is best*. You want just enough coil so you can be in the most ideal spot at the top of the backswing.

Preset Swing Plane at Eight O'Clock Position

Eight o'clock is a very important position for your glove hand. As your glove hand and arm swing back on an inside path from your left shoulder ball-and-socket joint and pass by your right leg, you post

Comfortable Resistance

When your glove hand starts back, a good thought as far as your lower body is concerned is to give yourself what I call *comfortable resistance*. That is, your lower body doesn't begin to coil too much, too soon. By creating comfortable resistance, you are putting energy into your backswing. It is like stretching a rubber band. Now it is ready to fly.

your weight, and with the weight in position you can continue to coil around that post you've created. You continue to reach back and allow your left side to go leisurely with the flow. Four things have to occur at eight o'clock:

1. Reach back to get your glove hand even with your toe line, go back inside.

2. Establish your weight on your right foot.

3. Coil enough so that your left shoulder is in line with the ball or slightly behind the ball.

4. Allow your head to go slightly back with the flow. How far back is slightly back? The limit is that the right ear should not go beyond the inside of the right shoe.

Let me add one more thought at eight o'clock. As you reach back with your glove hand, think about shaking hands with someone. Do this without a club in your hand. While at eight o'clock look at your glove hand, with fingers extended and hand straight. Put your hand at knife edge to the ground. Now tilt it back just 20 degrees. You should now be in a better position to shake hands. This is the angle that you want your glove hand to be in at eight o'clock, when you put a club in your hand. (I'm working with your 7-iron.) You swing from your shoulder on an inside path. Once you've reached eight

Glove hand at eight o'clock position, where weight should be posted over the right foot.

o'clock, and you've got your four checkpoints, you are now 85 percent finished with your backswing, and you haven't even begun to swing up yet.

There are two important factors to these checkpoints:

1. When your left shoulder is over the ball at eight o'clock, it is now in position to take advantage of its ball-and-socket joint and swing up freely and easily. Many nonschooled golfers try to swing up into the backswing before they have coiled enough to get their left shoulder over the ball. The result is a short backswing and no power.

2. Your glove hand is in a "shake hands" position, tilted back 20 degrees to lay the shaft of your club back 20 degrees from your target line. This sets your clubhead behind your hand at eight

o'clock with the toe of the club pointing straight up. When all is as it should be at this moment, you are presetting your swing plane, and from here good things can happen. Eight o'clock is, again, a very important position.

Remember that up to now we have just gone back to eight o'clock, and we are working with a 7-iron in hand. Each time you attach your glove hand to the club, follow the same checkpoints. Also, as I guide you through these drills, try to maintain a consistent medium-firm grip pressure at all times.

Extension Tip

Before you start back, if you were to draw a line from the clubhead up to your left shoulder it would look close to a straight line, with no

Presetting the swing plane at the eight o'clock position by laying the club shaft back 20 degrees from the target line.

Tour Player Advice

U.S. Open champion Corey Pavin: "You want to think of your swing as following your track. You want your degree of angle to be the same all the time. When your swing plane is in the right place you will hit it as far as possible."

1986 U.S. Amateur Public Links champion, 1987 Amateur champion, and PGA Tour winner Billy Mayfair: "The way Glenn explains the proper position at the top of the backswing and the way he positions his students helps their feel and awareness. The student understands where he's coming from because they feel it and see it. Through Glenn's guided repetitions the student becomes more aware of the feel and the position of the glove hand."

Masters champion Craig Stadler: "I think you need to put a mental picture of just taking it back slow. If you get quick, you create a lot of unwanted problems."

hinge in the wrist area. If you were to draw a line from the clubhead to your left shoulder as you reach back to eight o'clock, it should also appear close to straight. No hinge has occurred in your left wrist as you've reached back to eight o'clock. Having done this, you have created a full swing arc. When you increase the swing arc, you increase clubhead speed. What you want is straight and comfortable, extension without tension. Don't lock up, and don't be stiff.

Eight O'Clock Drill

To get good at the left side controlling the swing, start by swinging the club back to eight o'clock and hold it. While holding it here, check your position and feel your weight. Do this over and over again to build muscle memory.

Make sure you reach back with your glove hand, away from your target on an inside path as if you are going to shake hands with someone. The back of your glove hand will be even with your toe line. When this is done properly, the clubface will fan open slowly and smoothly as you go back. When you are at eight o'clock, the toe of the club will be straight up in the air, and your shaft will be back 20 degrees from your target line. There is no hinging of the wrist at this time. Your left shoulder is over the ball, which has exposed your back to the target. You've allowed your head to go back slightly and you've posted your right hip weight over your right shoelaces. Once you can feel and duplicate this position, then you are ready to go up into the backswing.

The Still Head: Center of the Swing

In the last lesson we said that if you understand and can duplicate where your glove hand lands in the finish in relationship to where the target is, you will be better able to have a still head.

What I do as a teacher is take a still head and build a swing around it. Having said that, as we go into the backswing, there is an exception to the still head rule. It is okay for your head to go slightly back on the backswing, as indicated in step 4 in the sequence. Again, the limit is that your right ear should never go past the inside of your right foot.

This limit keeps you from having head sway and helps keep the swing in balance. No matter where you are in the golf swing, your upper body weight should stay between your two feet. We allow the head to go back slightly because it has weight and we want all of the weight behind the ball. In addition, allowing the head to go back slightly with the flow enables you to have a more comfortable and full backswing. Don't lead or lean with the head, but allow it to go back with the flow.

As you start your backswing, initially your head remains still, with your face square to the ground and looking toward the ball. Here's the sequence of movement as you go back. First your hand starts

Correct position at eight o'clock: the toe of the club is straight up in the air, shaft back 20 degrees, left shoulder over the ball, and weight posted over the right shoelaces.

back, as if you are going to shake hands with someone. This then causes the arm to go back, and then the left shoulder. As your upper body coils, allow your head to go back slightly with the flow when your left shoulder touches your chin.

Balancing Weight of the Swing

Think of a golf swing as a circle, and your head as the center of the circle. Compare this to a wheel on your car. If your wheels are out of balance, your steering wobbles. To correct this, automobile manufacturers place balancing weights on your wheels that cause the wheels to roll true, with no wobble. Think of your head as the balancing weight of your swing. If you keep your head still, your swing has a better chance of staying smooth. Every little movement of the head can lift, lower, or shift the entire swing circle. Excessive move-

Power Leak

In many cases with unschooled golfers, the right side tends to be a hindrance to a fluid backswing. If your right arm and right shoulder pick up (even subconsciously), this action causes your head to tilt to the left toward your target. This single flaw affects your balance, robs you of a full arc, and is a power leak.

ment can tilt the swing plane into all kinds of different positions, thus robbing your swing of repeatability. Golf legend Arnold Palmer adds, "The best thing I do is to keep my head in position throughout the process of the swing."

We have said that it is okay to allow your head to go slightly back with the flow of the backswing. With your head in the ideal position, you are strongly balanced with your weight behind the ball. We ask for a still head, but not a perfectly still head. Allow your head to go with the flow of your left hand, arm, and shoulder as they move into the backswing. But try not to allow your head to move up or down during the action. This will lead to a topped, or *fat*, shot. I like to think that if your head moves up or down more than two dimples on a golf ball, it has moved too much.

In 1982, a seventy-five-year-old gentleman came to me for golf lessons, and we got into a discussion about the still head. He told me that fifty years prior, he took a lesson in Scotland, and the pro at that time told him to "Hit and spit, hold your head position through the finish so that you can spit where the ball used to be." Nicklaus's former teacher used to hold his hair while he would swing a golf club. Your head and spine are the axis to the golf swing. If your head moves too much, then the whole swing is thrown out of balance. For example, if your head comes up during the downswing, it also pulls the clubhead up, which pulls the clubhead across the ball, causing a slice or a pull-hook, depending on the position of the clubface at impact.

Create a Full Swing Arc

Have you ever wished you could create a more full swing arc on your backswing? Have you ever thought of yourself as having tight muscles and tight tendons that would not allow you to go a little higher in the backswing with your glove hand? All you need to do is discover the gap in your left shoulder. This gap between your muscles and tendons gives you more swing freedom as you go into the backswing and upswing.

Most unschooled golfers have never heard of this gap, and they don't take advantage of it because they haven't been taught that the left side is the leader. One cause of a restricted backswing is that the right side gets too involved as you swing back and up. Here is what happens: the right arm pulls the left arm back too close to the vest (body), which locks up the left shoulder ball-and-socket joint.

The cure is achieved by teaching the right side to be a relaxed passenger. Reach back with the glove hand to a point where your left shoulder is even with the ball. You can then position your glove hand in the correct angle that will keep your left elbow from getting too close to the vest and locking up.

61

Shoulder Gap Drill

Here's a drill to show you that glove hand position plays a part in your being able to create a more full backswing. Reach back with

> **Use "Laser Beam" to Keep Head Still**
>
> Here's a fun exercise to help you keep your face from moving one way or the other. From the tip of your nose to the ball, think of a laser beam. While you go into the backswing and return to the ball, beam the ball with your nose as a pointer. When I caught up with PGA player John Morse on tour and shared this tip with him, he said, "That thought is good and can be a helpful practice tool on the range."

your glove hand (without a club in it), and have your hand in knife-edge position in relation to the ground. Have your glove hand at eight o'clock—arm fully extended and shoulder even with the ball. At this moment, you have a full shoulder coil. While in this position, rotate your glove hand so that your palm faces the sky. Now try to take your glove hand up to ten o'clock—you should feel that your left elbow is too close to your vest, and your left shoulder joint has limited range. Return your glove hand to eight o'clock, and this time rotate your glove hand to a point where it is facing the ground. Now take it up from your left shoulder. You should experience more range and will have found the gap. It is not necessary to have your palm to the ground to find the gap. What is recommended is that your glove is laid back just 20 degrees at eight o'clock. This sets your left elbow just a bit away from your body. In that position, you will have more range, a more full arc, more clubhead speed, and you will hit the ball farther.

From Eight O'Clock to Ten O'Clock: Wrist Hinge

Your glove hand is at eight o'clock and you have practiced all of your eight o'clock checkpoints. When you have coiled enough so your left shoulder is over the ball, you can take advantage of the left shoulder ball-and-socket joint and swing up to the top of the backswing. Think of yourself as in the clock again, and swing your glove hand and arm up from eight o'clock to ten o'clock. At ten o'clock pause and then start down. Ten o'clock is the transitional point between the back-swing and downswing.

It is between eight o'clock and ten o'clock that the wrist hinging occurs. As you use your left side muscles to push your glove hand up, gradually hinge your wrist so that the club shaft will be at a 90-degree angle to your forearm at ten o'clock. By the time your glove reaches ten o'clock the hinging should be complete, and you should be in a solid position with no wobbling or rocking.

Your glove hand tilt stays the same from eight o'clock up to ten o'clock. Keep in mind that at eight o'clock it is tilted back about 20 degrees in a "shake hands" position. As you go from 8 to 10 and hinge your wrist, the hand stays tilted back about 20 degrees. It is important that it doesn't tilt more or less on the way up, because it is controlling your swing plane. Your wrist hinges but doesn't change its tilt angle. The result is that when you are at ten o'clock your shaft is tilted back about 20 degrees. At the top of the backswing, your glove hand lies back about 20 degrees, laying the shaft back about 20 degrees, and that defines your swing plane. The angle of your glove controls the angle of your shaft, so the angle of your glove controls your swing plane.

The Slowest Part

The part between eight o'clock and ten o'clock is the slowest part of the golf swing. Never rush this area. By going slowly, you are better able to feel the hinge occurring. It is also easier to stop at ten o'clock with your glove hand, and your grip pressure can stay secure. These are all keys to better control as you go up into the backswing and start your transition back down from ten o'clock.

63

Compare a golf swing to a swing in the park. What happens as the seat of the swing is going up? It slows down on the way, reaches a still point, and then starts down slowly and gradually builds speed. Think of your arms as the chain or rope holding the seat of the swing, and think of your glove hand as the seat. As you swing your glove hand up, it should gradually slow down until it has a slight pause at the top (ten o'clock), and then start down slowly and gradually pick up speed, just like the swing in the park.

When your glove hand is at ten o'clock, your shoulder is over the ball and you have a 90-degree angle between your left forearm and the golf shaft. At this moment, your shaft will be at a 45-degree angle to the ground. At 45 degrees you are more in control of your clubhead and shaft than if it was parallel to the ground. This is the angle most good players want to feel.

Efrem Zimbalist Jr. demonstrating glove hand going up to ten o'clock and shaft tilted back near 20 degrees.

Keep in mind that we are doing a one-arm stop action exercise, and ten o'clock is where you always want to pause and come down from. You want to develop a feel for this spot (which I call the pocket). Once you start swinging, the motion will take you just a little farther. But even then you'll want to think about parking your glove hand (left hand for right-handed players) here. Now, if you were to position yourself so that your shaft was parallel to the ground at the top of the backswing during this exercise, experience tells me that the motion would cause you to overswing. Unless you have extraordinary skill, overswinging can open up a can of worms for mistakes. To help you to have more control, as you swing up, slow down as you go, park your glove hand at ten o'clock, pause, and then start down slowly.

Wrist Hinge Drill

Here's a drill for you: Hold the club only in your glove hand, and extend it out in front of you. While holding it there, hinge the wrist to get the club shaft straight up into the air.

The Speed Slot

The 20-degree shaft angle at the top of your backswing is what I call the *speed slot*. This is another example of the golf swing taking advantage of physics. When your swing plane is at or near 20 degrees, the clubhead will fly faster than if it were laid back 30 or 40 degrees.

You have just hinged your wrist to create a 90-degree angle between your left forearm and the club shaft. Now straighten it out and do it again—do you feel what muscles are activated to cause the hinge? It is those muscles that you use as you are hinging your wrist when you swing up from eight o'clock to ten o'clock. Once you are in the proper position at eight o'clock and you are ready to go up into the backswing you will notice that you have motion from your left

The author with PGA Senior Tour player Jim Ferree at a solid ten o'clock position: glove hand is at ten o'clock, left shoulder is over the ball, and there is a 90-degree angle between the left forearm and the club shaft.

shoulder as your glove hand goes up and that the motion of your wrist hinge is occurring simultaneously, in a slow, smooth manner.

At eight o'clock you have already set your weight in position and have coiled your upper body so that your left shoulder is even with or slightly behind the ball. From here, there is very little lower body motion. All that happens now is that your glove hand and arm go up from eight to ten o'clock. Your weight stays the same, for at eight o'clock you have established a counterbalanced situation. Your glove hand is on one side of your body and your left foot is on the other. As you go from eight to ten o'clock, you remain counterbalanced.

A big key while this is happening is that your right arm, shoulder, and back stay relaxed, hanging free with no tension or effort. You also have to guard against subconscious right side lifting.

Backswing Speed Control Drill

Take your 7-iron again, and just using your left side muscles swing back to eight o'clock with your glove hand reaching back until your left shoulder is over the ball. Keeping your left shoulder in that position, swing your glove hand up to ten o'clock (top of your backswing) in slow motion. Then bring it back down to eight o'clock. Now swing it up twice as fast as before. Let's say you just went up at 10 miles per hour. Take it up one more time, this time at 30 m.p.h. Next time, take it up slowly again. In your true golf swing, slow is the feeling you want.

The point of the drill is that you could take it up at whatever speed I ask for. How could you do that? You could because your mind is connected to the muscles you are using to do the job. This is what you want to do when you practice and play golf. By knowing what muscles you are using and by concentrating on using those muscles, you can control the speed. On the backswing, go the same slow speed each time and you will be on the way to a better swing.

The backswing is very awkward and unnatural to most new players and high handicappers. They create problems for themselves because the right hand and arm become involved and either pull the left hand off of its track or pick the left hand up too fast too soon. When that occurs they have lost their swing plane and their tempo, and have robbed themselves of a full arc.

Here's how I deal with this problem. In the beginning, work just with the left side muscles. As you go through the backswing, monitor what is occurring with each body part. After each swing make any needed corrections in position until you can reproduce the action correctly every time.

You can gain a more full swing arc by stretching out as you work on the backswing. If you can just stretch out a little each time you practice, that will increase your swing arc and your clubhead speed.

Also, remember to stay relaxed with the right side. Pay attention to the upper body coil, making sure to get your left shoulder over the ball and your weight and balance in the correct position. Monitor your glove hand grip pressure as well, maintaining consistent grip pressure all through the swing.

Learning a golf swing is a lot like sneaking up on something. It takes forever to get there, but once you are there—you're there. Go through the motions enough times so you can feel the positions, the motion, and the muscles doing the action. These muscles get stronger with every repetition.

Level Left Shoulder Coil: Big Key to the Backswing

Say I measured from your left shoulder to the ball as you stood over it with the club in your glove hand, and that distance was sixty-two inches. As your glove reaches back to eight o'clock and your shoulder is over or even with the ball, if I measure the distance again it should still be sixty-two inches. Your glove swings from eight to ten o'clock, and as you hold it at the top, if I were to measure the dis-

> ## The Pocket: Key to Better Rhythm
>
> As you swing your glove hand up to the top of the backswing, remember that you are swinging it up into an imaginary pocket at the top. You want to feel the same pocket and the same glove hand angle as you go to that spot. By going to exactly ten o'clock each swing, with every club, your swing will always have the same measurement (your glove will fly the same distance with each swing). This is a key to better rhythm.

tance from your left shoulder to the ground I should again get sixty-two inches. You swing your glove hand back down to seven o'clock and I measure once more and I get the same measurement, sixty-two inches. I talk with many pros on the tour and as they are on the driving range preparing for a tournament. I ask them, "What are you practicing on, what is your swing thought?" The players tell me over and over that they are working on a level left shoulder coil. As they reach back with their glove hand, they want to draw their left shoulder back even with the ground. So what you want also is a level left shoulder coil.

Here's what you must overcome to achieve this important move. You must learn to keep your right arm, hand, shoulder, and right side of your back relaxed. Seventy-five percent of all of the golfers practicing at this minute have never heard of a level left shoulder coil or how to practice that action. They have never been taught left side control. Remember the left side is the leader, the right side is the follower. The left side controls the swing and the right side goes for the ride. The left side is the authority and the right side is relaxed so it can just go with the flow of the action caused by the left side.

For those who do not have this knowledge it is very difficult to swing with a level left shoulder coil. This is because most people are right-handed, and the right hand has been getting them through life. In the unschooled golf swing it just naturally wants to help out. The problem with that is, the way we are built as humans, if the right shoulder picks up, the left shoulder drops. And if the left shoulder drops, you will lose the level left shoulder coil. Your left shoulder cannot stay level if your right side gets involved and picks up. This is one big reason the unschooled golfer is slow to become a better player. You must practice relaxation on the right side and stay focused on each swing so that the right side doesn't get tight, pick up, or get involved. Try to achieve relaxation on every swing you take.

Hold the club gently with your right hand. Think about relaxing the right arm and shoulder and treating the backswing as if you are doing a one-arm exercise. Remember, too, as you coil back, to keep your left knee level to the ground. Too much left knee flex would also cause your left shoulder to drop, collapsing your swing.

Backswing Review

To repeat the same backswing position every time, keep the right side out of it. Put your thinking in the back of your glove hand. What I look for at the top of the backswing is the following:

1. Glove at ten o'clock (left arm feels straight and comfortable— extension without tension).

2. Back of glove even with toe line.

3. A 90-degree angle between left forearm and club shaft, which is your original source of power, or leverage.

4. Your glove hand lies back near 20 degrees, which gives you the proper swing plane.

These four positions and the proper weight distribution create a position I call the *loaded gun*.

Think of the backswing as being part of your aim. It is similar to an archer pulling the bowstring back. Go back slowly, feel the correct position, and then start down.

Downswing Through Impact: Control the Power Angle

You are set up in the backswing and you are ready to start the downswing. The best advice as you start down is to start down slowly. Control the action with your left side, while you stay passive or relaxed with your right. Put your thinking in your glove hand. The first thing to remember is to keep your head and left shoulder still. Keep the left shoulder ball-and-socket joint in position—don't move it down or toward your target as you start your glove hand down.

As you swing your glove hand down from your left shoulder, think of bringing it straight down as if gravity were pulling it down. While you are doing this, control your angles on the way down. Because you didn't change your 20-degree glove hand angle at seven o'clock, the clubhead is slightly behind your hand on the way down. (See Figure 3.1.) You kept your 90-degree wrist hinge angle all the way into seven o'clock, so now the clubhead has that angle to release from as you swing through the ball. That's what puts the sting on the ball.

I want to show you something interesting. Lay a golf club on the ground pointing to one o'clock in the field to represent an inside-out

70

Four Keys to Creating a Full Swing Arc

At eight o'clock:

1. Weight on your right foot.
2. Left shoulder over the ball.
3. Head allowed to go slightly back.
4. Keep left arm extended with no hinging in the wrist area until after eight o'clock.

If any of these factors are not present, your clubhead will not generate its maximum speed.

swing path. Now, swing your 7-iron up to the top of the backswing and bring it down again. Keep your head and left shoulder still and bring your glove hand straight down from your left shoulder. From ten o'clock down to nine o'clock no angles change—from nine o'clock down to eight o'clock no angles change—from eight o'clock to seven o'clock no angles change. If you have kept the 90-degree power angle between your left forearm and club shaft and if you have kept your glove hand laid back 20 degrees, then you have controlled your swing plane all the way down into seven o'clock. At this moment the shaft should be parallel to the ground and also looking at one o'clock in the field. Your swing path and your 7-iron shaft are parallel like railroad tracks both looking at one o'clock. It is at this time that you pick up the path with your glove hand (from your shoulder, using your left side back muscles). You swing

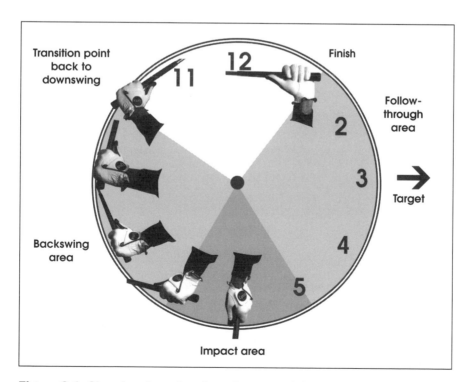

Figure 3.1 Glove hand coming down from ten o'clock to seven o'clock. Keep the 90-degree wrist hinge angle all the way to seven o'clock, so the clubhead has that angle to release from as you swing through the ball.

your glove hand toward one o'clock in the field. As you pick up your swing path with your glove hand and rotate it through, you will notice that your clubhead flies through on your inside-out swing path.

What has happened is that the angle you created at the top of the backswing (your swing plane) has come down, and now at seven o'clock it translates into your swing path. By doing this your clubhead is able to fly on one smooth outer circle. When it does that it also flies faster.

What we are talking about right now is what separates the amateurs from the pros. The pros have well-schooled golf swings. They

Advice from Two-Time U.S. Open Champion Ernie Els

Glenn: You're out here warming up, any major swing thoughts that you will use today as you practice?

Ernie: I played eighteen holes today already and didn't hit the ball that well. I'm coming off of a five-week holiday so I do have to work on a couple of things. My turn to the backswing is not all that good at the moment. I'm a little bit steep on it. I'm going to try to slide the clubhead away a little bit more and try to get my weight behind the ball instead of right over it. I'll work on those things.

Glenn: Once you've worked on those things, if someone would give you a compliment, what would you most like to hear?

Ernie: You're back on plane. Normally when I hit my backswing in fine shape the rest of it will take care of itself. I'll be happy if someone tells me my backswing is beautiful.

Glenn: Once you know your swing and you have the proper mechanics, then you go out and practice and you get timing through that?

Ernie: Exactly.

understand and are able to control their angles. But most amateurs have never had these angles explained to them and don't know how to control them. When first learning how to control these angles, it is best to move slowly so you can better feel what is taking place. As I said earlier, first you build a racetrack and then you race. Walk yourself through the positions feeling and monitoring yourself. If you feel comfortable and in control at a certain speed, then gradually increase the speed. You must control the speed—don't let the speed control you. Controlling your angles increases your clubhead speed through impact. The pro speed is 110 m.p.h. and more, the amateur speed is 95 m.p.h. and less. This is a big reason why pros play better golf. The quickest way to learn to control these angles is to learn left side control. The left side is the leader and the right side is the follower. When you attach the right side, keep it relaxed and let it go with the flow.

Two Downfalls: Curiosity and Anxiety

There are two words that are the downfall of many a would-be good golfer. The first word is *curiosity*. Many unschooled golfers want to look and see the ball fly before they hit it, or they react to the hit before it happens and their head comes up. Or they don't trust their swing coming down and are afraid they will hit the ground, so they lift their head and body to avoid a shock to their system.

When we talked about going up into the finish, I said that if you understand and can duplicate where your glove hand lands in the finish in relationship to your target, you are better able to keep your head still. I asked you to keep your head still until all swinging parts are completed and you are holding your finish. By giving you that advice, I planted the seed to help you not to be so curious. Believe me, you have to practice and rehearse each swing and focus on not being curious to correct this error. The King, Arnold Palmer, says, "The best thing I do in golf is keep my head in position throughout the process of the swing." There are many blind golfers, and good ones. Sight

PGA Tour player Tom Purtzer demonstrates glove hand at nine o'clock swinging down to a solid seven o'clock position. Keep the 90-degree power angle between your left forearm and club shaft and keep your glove hand laid back 20 degrees to control your swing plane all the way down into seven o'clock.

is not needed to hit the ball, but keeping your head in position is. Consider this: a golf swing takes about 1.3 seconds, and the golf ball flies for 3 to 9 seconds. That gives you plenty of time to take a look after holding your finish in a balanced position.

The second word that is the downfall of many a would-be good golfer is *anxiety*. The unschooled golfer is in too much of a hurry to go up and down in the backswing. This huge flaw can in most cases be traced to the right arm wanting to help out or become involved. As golfers, we have to learn to be passive with the right side. This takes time, concentration, and practice. The right side always wants to get involved. The problem is that as it gets too involved too soon and pushes against the shaft on the way down, it can throw your angles out of position: it pushes your clubhead outside of your ball, and it crosses your lines. This is called *coming over the top*.

Railroad Track Drill

Do you want to have some fun with your friends? Here's a drill you can do. Stand behind a player ten feet or so, looking at the target. Ask the player to take the swing up to the top of the backswing and hold it. Now with your right hand as a pointer trace the player's glove hand as he swings down. Do it again, and this time also trace the clubhead down using your left hand as a pointer. If your hands and arms don't cross as the player comes down, he is controlling his angles. Your pointing fingers come down parallel like railroad tracks.

While doing this, have the player swing down in slow motion. If your hands and arms cross each other on the way down, his clubhead has gotten in front of his glove hand and his glove hand angle has changed because of right side involvement or anxiousness. As a player, it is important to keep the clubhead a bit behind your glove hand on the way down and not to cross your lines.

As your glove hand swings up from eight o'clock to ten o'clock, you create the 90-degree wrist hinge angle. For maximum power you keep that angle as you swing your glove hand all the way down to seven o'clock. But what if the right side gets anxious, pushes at nine o'clock, and opens up that angle? Well, that is where most of your power has been thrown, and by the time you get to the ball, you've lost the sting. The same thing occurs if you push it open at eight o'clock. You must try to keep your right side passive and control your angles all the way down to seven o'clock with your left side muscles and your glove hand to have a powerful swing.

Seven O'Clock: Accelerate Through Impact

As you swing your glove hand down from ten o'clock, at seven o'clock the glove hand is not going down anymore but is now swinging through the bottom of the swing. Your glove hand is entering the impact area. At this time three things happen, but they have to happen in the sequence I'm going to tell you.

1. It is now as you pick up the swing path from your left shoulder, pulling through with the powerful muscles of the left side of your back, that you begin to pull your glove hand toward one o'clock in the field.

2. Rotate the left hand and forearm a quarter turn.

3. Accelerate through the ball and into the finish.

Path, rotate, accelerate. The action happens at seven o'clock, and it must happen in that order.

You are accelerating through the ball, not down on the ball. Granted when your glove hand is coming down from ten o'clock, that is the momentum gathering area, but it is not pedal to the metal. At the top of the backswing, you have created a loaded gun. It is at seven o'clock that you pull the trigger—accelerating your glove hand by directing and pulling it with your left side muscles.

Remember that at seven o'clock you have controlled your angles so at this time your club shaft is parallel to the ground and looking at one o'clock in the field (slightly right of target). The clubhead appears just a bit behind your glove hand and is now in position to release from the inside. This is the only swing path that will put the type of spin on the ball that makes it the most ballistic, allowing it to fly farther. Here's another benefit: the golf ball that flies right to left (a draw) is less affected by the wind.

Think of a speedometer. Ten o'clock, the top of the backswing, is where your glove hand starts down. At this moment your glove hand has made a slight pause and is at zero miles per hour. The finish is 120 m.p.h. As your glove hand starts down, it is gradually picking up speed—0, 10, 20, 30, 40, 50, 60 m.p.h. When it reaches seven o'clock you accelerate through the ball and up into the finish—70, 80, 90, 100, 110, and 120 m.p.h. As you pull through the ball and up into the finish with your glove hand, that is where the ripping starts. As power-hitting British Open and PGA champion John Daly says, "Grip it and rip it!"

Tom Purtzer demonstrates the clubhead slightly behind glove hand as he goes from the eight o'clock position to the seven o'clock position. The clubhead is ready to release from the 90-degree wrist hinge power angle as he swings through the ball.

The Freeway On-Ramp

The moment of impact is the most sensitive part of the golf swing. Good players have good timing at this moment, and tour players have great timing through impact. The timing of what happens as your clubhead approaches the ball and as it swings through is a result of player control and practice. Your timing gets better the more you use your swing.

Here's another example of how you can control the regulation of speed, or timing, of your glove hand. Imagine as you swing your glove hand down that it is on a ramp entering the freeway. Your glove hand reaches a point when it is not swinging down anymore, but it is swinging through the impact area. It is at that point (seven o'clock) that you are now on the freeway. This is when you step on the gas and accelerate through the impact area. You've got to get on the freeway—the swing path—before you step on the gas. The acceleration at the bottom of the swing can also be compared to a race car coming out of a turn, as described in the sidebar on pages 79–80.

Right Arm Relaxation: Key to a Free Swing

The challenge to the new golfer and the high handicapper is to keep the right arm out of the swing, to keep it relaxed. Most people are right-handed, and the right side will always naturally want to get involved. What you want is a slow, smooth backswing. If the right side gets involved it can cause these errors:

1. Right side tension can change the swing from smooth to abrupt and jerky.

2. It puts right side/left side muscle conflict into the swing.

3. It could change the clubface position and cause it to jump track (go off of the arc).

78

Right Arm Relaxation Drill

Place a folded towel under your right arm. Hold it there in a relaxed manner. With both hands gripping the club, reach your glove hand back and on an inside path as if you are reaching back to shake hands with someone. Reach back to eight o'clock. When your glove hand is at eight o'clock, your right arm should still be holding the towel in a relaxed fashion. As you push up with your left side muscles from eight to ten o'clock this will cause the right arm to have a little sep-

Know Where You Are Going

Put your thinking in the back of your glove hand. Always have a clear picture in your mind as to where your glove hand is going to land in the finish, and don't stop until you reach the top. Keep ripping it up to the finish.

aration, only because your glove hand is swinging up, not because of any right side effort.

When you are at the top of the backswing at ten o'clock, your right hand and wrist should remain free and relaxed, as should the muscles of your right shoulder and back. Your right arm should be so relaxed that you have the feeling the weight of your elbow joint is just hanging down due to gravity. Your right hand is comfortably attached and the thumb of your glove hand should be in the crease of the right palm. (Attachment of the right hand is covered in Chapter 4.) There should be no gap between your two hands, no separation. If at ten

Dudley Hart on the Race Car Analogy

I had the following conversation with 1998 World Open champion and four-time All-American Dudley Hart about the race car analogy.

Glenn: Tell me what you think about this analogy. Think of the path that your glove hand travels on as a racetrack, and think of your glove hand as a race car. As your glove hand comes down, it reaches a point where it isn't coming down anymore, but going through the impact area. The area the glove hand passes through from downswing to through-swing we can call the corner of the racetrack.

As your glove hand comes down, you gradually build up speed and continue to build speed through the corner, then once you are through the corner, it is at that moment you accelerate your glove hand or step on the gas.

Dudley: Exactly. If you step on the gas right from the top, then you'll get off the track, lose control. As you said, Glenn, coming down is the momentum gathering area. It is going to be smooth and

continued

then I rip. Because if I rip from the top, it will be all right hand and right shoulder, which I try to avoid.

Glenn: Can you, by working on the timing of your acceleration, give your swing extra speed if the situation warrants it?

Dudley: Yes, that would be a controlled increase in speed which is hard for some people to understand. It takes a while to learn. But you have to be aware of when to exactly speed it up and not do it too soon or you spin out.

Glenn: In 1989 I went to Skip Barber Race School to learn how to drive and race Indy cars. All racers know you must have controlled speed going into the corner or you don't come out of the corner. As you are coming out of the corner, the nose of your race car must see or be looking at the racetrack before you step on the gas. My question is, could we think of the butt end of the club as the nose of the race car and be aware that it is looking at the target before we step on the gas and accelerate through the impact area?

Dudley: That is a good analogy. I like that idea. The nose of the race car must be in the correct position before you go pedal to the metal. As you know, Glenn, there are always a lot of ways to explain certain things to people. You could say the same thing six different ways. If you say that to some people they might get a good picture, idea, and thought. They might say, "Oh, yeah, now I understand." A great analogy. It is important to be able to get your point across to different people. It is important to express swing thoughts in many different ways. My father is a golf pro, and he is the one that has taught me my whole life, and he was very good at that. He would find a way for me to be able to pick up on the correct action. It is hard to explain what it is in someone's head that some examples click. Each golfer will always learn as they go.

o'clock your hands are not comfortably molded together, you can bet your right side is too tight.

Swing your golf club up into the backswing. Park your glove hand at ten o'clock. Hold it there. Take time to feel a relaxed right arm. To check your position rotate your head, but don't pick it up.

Right Arm During Downswing

A lot has been written about the action of the right elbow on the downswing. The way I teach, you don't even have to think about it and it will still be in the ideal position.

Your thought should be to keep the right arm relaxed and control the downswing with your glove hand and left arm. Provided that you control your angles on the way down, if the right arm remains passive, the right elbow will be in the proper position. I know through research that this occurs. If you tried to think of what the right elbow does on the downswing, the result would be left side/right side conflict, which would rob your swing of speed and smoothness.

81

Know what to do with your left side and allow your right side to go with the flow. This needs to be rehearsed many times because human nature dictates that the right side should be involved. As soon as it enters the picture, it can cause many swing errors.

The right arm stays relaxed on the downswing. Your first move down from the proper position at the top of the backswing is of utmost importance. You had better stay relaxed with that right side. Start your glove hand down gradually so you can feel the control of your glove hand. By controlling the hinge of your left wrist and the angle of your glove hand as you swing it down from your left shoulder, you will keep the relaxed right arm and elbow in the ideal position as you come down and begin to pull through impact. By left side control and right side relaxation, again, you take left side/right side conflict out of the equation.

Efrem Zimbalist Jr. demonstrating relaxed right arm. Control the downswing with your glove hand and left arm, and allow your right side to go with the flow.

Tour Player Advice

U.S. Open champion Corey Pavin: "You want to think of your swing as following your track. You want your degree of angle to be the same all the time. When your swing plane is in the right place you will hit it as far as possible."

1986 U.S. Amateur Public Links champion, 1987 Amateur champion, and PGA Tour winner Billy Mayfair: "The way Glenn explains the proper position at the top of the backswing and the way he positions his students helps their feel and awareness. The student understands where he's coming from because they feel it and see it. Through Glenn's guided repetitions the student becomes more aware of the feel and the position of the glove hand."

Masters champion Craig Stadler: "I think you need to put a mental picture of just taking it back slow. If you get quick, you create a lot of unwanted problems."

4

GRIP: GLOVE HAND CONTROLS, RIGHT FOLLOWS

The golf swing begins the moment you grasp the club. Learn the proper balance between the right and the left hand and play efficiently. Many top pros agree this is one of the most important parts of the golf swing. A golf swing will improve more quickly if it begins with a good grip.

The proper grip pressure will help in many ways:

1. It creates a free-flowing swing.

2. It helps with right-side body relaxation.

3. It promotes the initial alignment of the clubface to the intended flight of the ball.

4. It helps return the clubface to proper alignment at impact.

5. It enhances the timing of the release.

6. It enables the hands to hinge properly throughout the swing.

Proper grip and grip pressure also allow you to achieve maximum clubhead speed through the ball and into the finish. Your grip is your direct connection to what happens at impact. Wherever the back of your glove hand goes, so goes the clubface. Remember, the clubface is an extension of the back of your glove hand. Thus, the glove hand is the central control of your golf swing. A good player puts his or her thinking into the back of the glove hand.

Proper Equipment for a Good Grip

To help you attain a good grip, before we examine the grip in detail, have your local pro check the grips on your clubs for the following:

1. Make sure they are not too old, worn out, or slick.

2. Make sure your grips are in the proper alignment to the clubface.

3. See if you can find a grip you like with an alignment aid.

Also, I recommend that you wear a full-finger leather golf glove. As I mentioned earlier, a golf glove acts as adhesion between the grip and your hand. It helps you hold on better and serves as a reminder which hand is the primary gripping hand.

Now that we've covered the grips on your clubs and the necessity of utilizing a glove, we're ready to put our glove hand (left hand for the right-handed player) on the grip first.

84

Simon Hobday on the Importance of Grip
Simon Hobday, 1994 Senior U.S. Open champion, commented, "You have to grip the club correctly. If you don't, it's like owning an expensive rifle with the sights out. You can't hit anything. You've got to have your sights right before you fire."

Glove Hand

While we are talking about the glove or left hand, there are a couple of checkpoints I'd like you to examine. First, choke down on the club just enough so when you look across the top of your left hand you can see the butt of the club sticking out. It's important that you understand why.

Look at the way a grip is tailored. It is narrower at the bottom and wider at the top or butt of the club. If you have the wide part showing during the swing, it will help your left hand to stay firm through the hitting area. During a swing, the clubhead will create centrifugal force, and this force wants to pull the club out of your hand. Showing the butt of the club enables you to use this force to your advantage in pressing the grip against your hand, helping your grip strength. The result is solid contact and longer ball flight.

A weak grip is often a key reason for a bad shot. If you lose the butt of the club in your glove hand, the speed of the clubhead can actually make your grip weaker. Also, showing an inch or slightly less than an inch of the butt of the club as you place your glove hand on it places your hands closer to the balance point on the club. This will give you more control and will increase your percentage of good shots.

The second checkpoint is how the grip lies in your palm. On the palm of your hand, you have a thumb pad and a pad below the little finger which forms the heel of the hand. There is a crease between the two pads in your palm. The grip of the club should never lie in between these two pads. It should cross your hand where the fingers meet the palm so that if you hold the club straight out with your left hand, the heel pad will rest on top of the grip. You should be able to hold the club with your little finger and the heel pad of your glove hand. This tells me that as you hold the club, it is settled properly in your glove hand.

Another visual that two-time Masters champion Ben Crenshaw shared with me is to think of where the fingers come into the palm as the root of the fingers—we can also call that area the first crease.

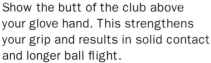

Show the butt of the club above your glove hand. This strengthens your grip and results in solid contact and longer ball flight.

The club should lie at the root of the last three fingers, not in the crease of the palm.

You want the club to lie across the root of the last three fingers on your left hand.

The major gripping fingers in the golf grip are the last three fingers of the left hand for the right-handed player or the last three fingers of the right hand for the left-handed player. This is another reason I think a full-fingered glove will make your grip more secure.

When you place your left thumb on the club, place it slightly to the right of center on top of the grip, causing the "V" on the crease between thumb and index finger to point between your neck and right shoulder. This is what we call a *neutral grip*. Employ a controlled firmness and avoid the white-knuckle death grip, which former Golf Channel host Peter Kessler calls the "White Knuckle Special."

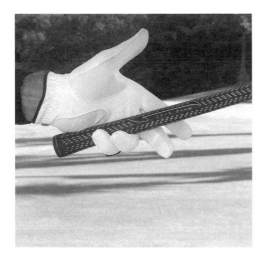

Club fits underneath bottom pad. The little finger is one of the major grippers of the glove hand.

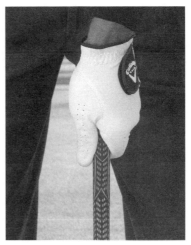

Most pros operate with a neutral grip as shown, and it's this one that I recommend.

What Is Ideal Glove Hand Strength?

Hold the club as firmly as you can, strongly enough so that you feel solid contact with the club throughout the swing but not so firm as to put tension in the left wrist. Tension in the left wrist will take away your ability to release the clubhead with full speed at the proper time. Ideally, the grip strength will be firm enough so there is no slippage of the fingers, yet not so tight as to create tension.

Try this demonstration. Drop a ball on the cement and see how it rebounds. A golf ball is designed to rebound from a solid surface. If you have a firm grip with your left hand, it will enhance the possibility of striking the ball with a solid clubface, producing a solid ball flight. Now drop a ball in the grass. The ball will barely hop from the surface because it hit something softer. If your right hand is too tight, it weakens the left hand grip, and the ball is contacted by a weak surface, which means less distance. A solid grip with your glove hand will equal solid contact.

Glove Hand Strengthening Drill

I like to give my students this exercise to help them strengthen the left hand. Get a racquet ball and keep it handy at home, possibly near your favorite chair. Squeeze it with your left hand and hold it firmly for a slow five count and then relax your hand. Doing ten repetitions at a time is enough. If you can squeeze it each evening, you'll build up strength and put the focus on the left hand. But remember to squeeze the ball with the left hand only (right hand for left-handed players). This will help develop a passive right hand that will not overpower your left.

Right Hand: The Vardon Grip

The right hand is a position hand, not a strength hand. The main focus with the right hand should be to place it on the club in the proper position. Tour legend Sam Snead (who was voted Best Golf Swing of the [Twentieth] Century by golf writers) told me, "Put your right hand on the club as if you're holding a bird. You don't want to hurt the bird, but you don't want the bird to get away." To keep your hands from showing any separation during the swing, think of your glove hand, thumb, and golf club as the bird. Ken Venturi, 1964 U.S. Open champion, was once told by a teacher that it would take him two years to learn to have a gentle, relaxed pressure with his right hand.

If the right hand is too tight, it's like trying to push a car with the brakes on. It simply wastes energy. If I were to assign pressure to each hand, I'd give the left hand 85 percent strength and the right hand only 15 percent. The more relaxed you are with the right hand, the more control you will have with the left, and the greater release the clubhead will have through the ball. In other words, the proper grip pressure will produce more clubhead speed, which will produce more distance.

One more point on pressure. If your right hand is too tight, it will break down the strength of the left hand during impact, causing both hands to become weak. If you have ever had a club spin in your hands during impact, you can bet your right hand was too tight.

Most amateurs, no matter how they are taught, will always have a tendency to be too tight with their right hand. One reason I teach 85 percent strength in the left and only 15 percent with the right is because of that tendency. A too-tight right hand will impede the release of the clubhead and push the shaft off of plane. This is one cause for going over the top at the start of the downswing.

To teach the right hand to be more passive, I start with grip pressure. When a golfer thinks 15 percent and it gets a little tighter, the right hand grip may still be passive enough to get a good result, but if the golfer thinks 50 percent and it gets tighter, that often becomes the cause of errors in swing mechanics.

Right-Hand Grip Pressure Drill

Pick up a golf ball in your right hand. Take it back as if to throw it, but don't throw. Now look at how you are holding the ball. Most people would hold the ball with their fingers, and not in the palm. The reason is that this gives your wrist more freedom. While you are holding the ball there, move your wrist back and forth but don't drop the ball. On a scale from 1 to 10 (10 meaning you'll crush the ball and 1 being you'd drop it), you should feel that you are holding it with

89

Grip 85 Percent with Left Hand, 15 Percent with Right

Grip pressure varies among the top players—but for new and high handicap players gripping 85 percent with the left hand and 15 percent with the right has proven to be advantageous. It is my recommendation that even top players give this a try, for those who do are more powerful and hold up under pressure.

the pressure of a 2 or 3. Try this. As you rock your wrist back and forth, gradually tighten your grip on the ball. What you will discover is that the tighter you squeeze the less wrist freedom you have. The same thing happens during your golf swing. The tighter you hold the club with your right hand the less freedom your right wrist has. This impedes the release of the clubhead and also takes away from the clubface's ability to return square behind the ball at impact. Ideally you want to feel that you are holding firmly enough so there is no slippage, but not so tight that you rob yourself of wrist freedom.

Right Hand Position

We've covered grip pressure in detail, and now we need to cover the proper right hand position, which is an equally important aspect to the golf grip.

What position do you want? First of all, you want the palm of your right hand to face the target. Placing your right hand on the golf club so that the palm faces the target could be the only natural thing about the swing. Put your hands in a praying position, then drop your left hand. You see that your right palm faces the target. This is natural. Take the time to have your clubface face the target, then when you attach your right hand, have it also face the target. By doing this, as you swing through impact, your right palm wants to return to its natural position, which is facing the target, and therefore it will automatically help the clubface break back square behind the ball at the moment of impact.

The thumb of your left hand fits in the crease between the two pads of your right hand. Now, should you employ the interlock or the overlap style of grip? I believe the most successful grip for every golfer is the overlapping Vardon grip. It's the only grip I teach, and I'll tell you why.

The little finger on the right hand lies over the top of the index finger of the left in the classic Vardon grip. This keeps the hands close

Right palm faces the target.   Glove thumb fits in crease of right hand.

together so they can act as one unit, allowing the clubhead to have the release you want for maximum power. The little finger should not lie in the crease between the first two fingers. Lay the finger over the top and keep it relaxed. Anytime during the swing, you should be able to flick it.

The Vardon grip was originated by Harry Vardon, who won the 1896, 1898, 1899, 1903, 1911, and 1914 British Opens. He also finished in second place four times. He won the U.S. Open in 1900, and placed second in 1913 and 1920. The vast majority of today's world-class tournament players use this grip. The Vardon grip is a rich part of golf tradition, and is over one hundred years old. If you look at the Vardon Trophy given each year to the PGA Tour player with the best stroke average on tour for the entire year, you will see a bronze replica of Harry Vardon's hands. If you look closely, you will be able to see the little finger of his right hand lying on top of the index finger of his left hand.

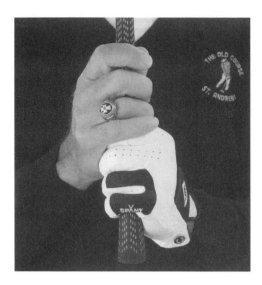

The Vardon grip. The little finger on the right hand lies over the top of the index finger of the left, enabling the hands to act together as one unit.

Here's how Harry Vardon himself described this position: "The little finger of my right hand rides on top of the first finger on my left hand." Lee Trevino has won five Vardon Trophies. Next time you see him swing, look closely at his little finger. It is exactly the same as Harry Vardon's.

Generally speaking, when the pressure of competition mounts during a round or during a tournament, the first part of the grip to tense up is the little finger on the right hand. This can cause the ball to drift to the right because it causes a split-second delay of the glove hand rotation, which prevents you from being able to work the clubhead through the ball. This, in turn, delays the clubhead rotation, which results in an open clubface at impact. Practice gentle pressure.

The two middle fingers of the right hand should have slight pressure on the grip. The index finger of the right hand can be thought of as a trigger finger on a gun. Hold your club straight out in front of you, point it at the target, and begin to think of the index finger of your right hand as a trigger finger. Your right thumb should be slightly over the top, just left of center, with the inside portion of the thumb touching the grip. The right thumb and index finger should not touch each other, but you should be able to pinch the grip slightly with these two fingers.

Try to keep the right thumb and index finger in position throughout the swing. The crease or "V" between the right thumb and index finger should point to an area between your neck and right shoulder. This position, when properly placed, will act like a saddle for your club at the top of the backswing and also in the finish position. The result will be that your swing will be more in control both at the top of the backswing and in the follow-through position.

Your swing will be easier to repeat because this grip helps reduce any excessive motion when you make the transition from backswing to downswing. The interlocking grip has more of a tendency to tighten during the swing. When this happens, the right forearm muscles tighten, and this alone can cause the release of the clubhead to be delayed. This creates a soft hit, resulting in lack of distance. A tight right hand also throws your timing off.

Remember, the left hand is your strength, your guide, and your central control. The right hand is important because of its position on the club. Put your thinking in your left hand and be aware through feel of the proper grip pressure. A tight right hand robs you of distance and accuracy.

93

 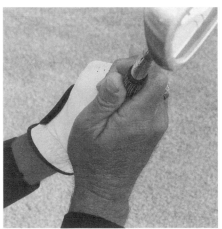

Right index finger and thumb form a saddle that helps to control the swing both at the top of the backswing and in the follow-through position.

Impact Through Finish Drill (Both Hands)

Now try the Impact Through Finish Drill described in Chapter 2 with both hands attached. As you are holding your finish, here are some key things to check for so that your right side shows no tension:

1. The little finger on your right hand should be so relaxed that someone could flick it.

2. Your right elbow should hang down showing no tension.

3. The right wrist should show a comfortable concave position rather than showing any form of tension.

Also, as you swing up into the finish with both hands, feel a slight comfortable pull between your elbows as you go up. This helps prevent your left elbow from flying left, which would cause you to break the glass wall and take your head out of position. As you hold your finish, the butt of the club is toward your target and so are your elbows. This is a classic target-oriented finish for a player hitting a draw.

Grip Review

Only through swinging a club enough times and flighting enough balls will you develop and be able to find the grip pressure for you that will allow your clubhead to generate its maximum speed.

CHECKPOINTS TO PRACTICE

1. Your glove hand must have controlled strength and stay solidly connected.

2. Your left wrist must have freedom.

3. Your right hand must hold gently throughout the swing with no slippage.

4. You must swing without tension in the right wrist.

This is what you strive for. Your clubhead can now fly its fastest. You can now launch your best shot.

As I teach new players, I position their left hand so that the "V" points between their neck and right shoulder. This is unnatural for them. The student will want to go to a more natural position, which is weak. It is important to check the glove hand position before you swing. Palms facing each other is natural and comfortable (in the praying position). In golf, when the left hand is positioned a little to the right of natural position, with the "V" pointing between the neck and the right shoulder, it will act as a loaded spring that will help automatically initiate the quarter turn. The result is that the clubface is more likely to return to the ball in a solid position at impact.

Now that we have built your swing from the waist up, in the next chapter we add the leg action.

Tournament Player Advice

Senior PGA Tour player Ken Still, winner of over one million dollars, says, "A good grip is like the steering wheel on your car. If you didn't have one, it would be difficult to go anywhere in a controlled manner."

PGA Tour star Jack Nicklaus, recalling the 1962 U.S. Open at Oakmont, said, "Pressure can catch you at the oddest times. Addressing the ball on the eighteenth tee on Sunday, I felt 1,000 percent confident I would hit a drive equally as fine as my previous day's beauty. However, while I was swinging down into the ball my right hand suddenly decreed otherwise."

PGA Tour player Billy Ray Brown advises, "Your right hand is important because of the position that you put it on the golf club once you set it properly. Set it and forget it. From there on everything is controlled by your glove hand."

PGA Tour player and U.S. Open champion Payne Stewart said, "With the right hand, don't choke the chicken."

5

LEG ACTION: GO WITH THE FLOW

With good upper body motion, the legs follow properly. So pull the string and be on target. I have found that if you can increase golfers' awareness of where their body parts are throughout the golf swing, you will automatically increase their reflex control and sharpen their hand-eye coordination. Understanding and being able to perfect the finest parts of the golf swing adds up to the clubface traveling true and fast.

In a recent conversation with PGA Tour player Chip Beck, I asked him to give me his thoughts on the leg action during the swing. "The way I feel about the legs, they do work in the swing," he said. "But if the upper body works properly, the legs will support the swing and they will work properly." This wisdom is the modern day thinking of many of the world's greatest golfers, who could get down on their knees and still hit the ball nearly 250 yards. When I build a golf swing, I build it from the waist up first. Only when the rest is properly put together do I add the leg action. Think of the first few lessons that we have had as building a sentence. Now we are ready to punctuate. Where does the punctuation come in the sentence? On the

Head still, glove hand at four o'clock, and with good upper body motion, the right side goes with the flow.

end of the sentence. So where do the legs come in the swing? On the end of the swing.

When you take your start position, ideally you return to that position at impact. They say perfect timing in the golf swing is when your glove hand and belt buckle return to where they began at address.

Before adding the legs, it's important that I give you one thought about your head. Even though we've said the head can move slightly back with the backswing, when you begin the downswing, concentrate on not moving your head down. Try to keep the field of vision from your eyes to the ball consistent throughout your swing. Also, when your glove hand is picking up your swing path and moving toward the target, try to keep your head from going forward. Think of pulling your glove hand into and through a wall that keeps your left eye and left foot from moving forward. Start your glove hand down first, using your left side muscles, and then as you pull through impact let your lower body weight flow smoothly and solidly over to your left side.

The Brick Wall: A Review

At address, draw a line from your left eye to your left foot. Your head is the top of the wall and your left foot is the bottom of the wall. If either moves forward before your glove hand passes through the wall, the result will be a weak hit. Practice keeping your head still until you've finished your swing because your head will want to go naturally with the flow of the swing. How far forward can your head go after the hit? PGA Tour player Tom Purtzer provided an answer by saying, "No matter where you are in your golf swing, your upper body weight should remain between your two feet."

Belt Buckle and Knee Toward Your Target

Let's start by doing an exercise with your hands on your hips. Pick a target and stand with your feet shoulder width apart. Think of the target as twelve o'clock. To the right of the target is one o'clock, and to the left of the target is eleven o'clock. First, slowly and easily turn your body toward the target. While doing this, relax your right leg and allow it to comfortably go with the flow of the turn. Again start your belt buckle toward the target, but think of swinging it only to one o'clock. You've now moved your left hip weight solidly over your left foot. When you feel this, ease your right knee toward the target, comfortably using the muscles of your right hip joint. If you have done this properly, you should feel the weight easing off the right foot, but still remaining slightly on the inside edge of your right shoe. Now when your right knee goes toward the target you'll finish with most of your weight on the left foot and a balanced weight on the right toe area of your right foot.

If your right foot feels like it is grinding, mashing, or twisting on the ground, that tells me you are trying to make this move, but you still have too much weight on your right side. The reason for this move is to get your weight on the left side. Think of taking the right knee toward your target. Don't try to do something with your right foot. Let the right foot merely follow the knee.

If you don't finish with your weight on your left foot, you will lose power. Here is an example: If you throw a punch and fall back, it is not much of a hit. The same thing happens as you swing to the target. If you fall back onto the right side, away from the target, it is a weak hit. Finishing with your weight on your left side is a valuable ingredient to power.

Senior PGA Tour player and former Stanford University golf coach Bruce Summerhays says, "Move to the left side with concentrated power, not with speed. The key is to stay in control of your upper body angles. This is what contributes to full release through the ball."

To eliminate over-rotating your lower body, feel that you're taking your belt buckle only to the one o'clock position. By doing this you will be better able to hit the draw. This will also keep your right heel from spinning out as you go into the finish. When you are holding your finish with your weight on your left foot and your right toe is helping you balance, it is okay for your right heel to be straight up or a little laid back from the target line, but try to avoid having it fall out across the target line. I see this flaw on both the pro and amateur levels. It usually results from lower body over-rotation. Depending on blade position at impact, you'll either pull hook or hit a big slice.

Now try that same exercise, but this time keep your head from moving forward or up and down. Bend forward from the waist as if you had a club in your hand. As your weight goes to your left, try not to lift your upper body. Stand with your hands on your hips and try to keep your head still. By keeping your head still, you will feel a slight comfortable arch in your back and most of your weight should be on your left foot. Your left leg is perpendicular to the ground and is now supporting your upper body. Check to see and feel that your left knee is not locked, but has a slight flex. Straight and comfortable is what you strive for. Your right toe becomes a balancing point. This is how you finish in a good golf swing.

Finish with your weight on your left foot and your right toe helping you balance. Avoid over-rotating and having the right heel fall out across the target line.

Right Leg Release

Why is the right leg release important? Your right leg weighs about one-fifth of your total body weight. In a golf swing, you have all the momentum of the swing going toward the target. If the right leg is not going with the flow of the action, then one-fifth of your weight would be holding back, causing a drag on your swing. In that case, you are not allowing yourself to swing as fast or smoothly as you can. So what we are trying to do is release the right leg and let it go with the flow of the swing. (One of the best golfers in the world at doing this is PGA Tour player Lanny Wadkins. Next time you see him, watch his release.) Compare this to a right-handed pitcher throwing a baseball. He winds up, throws the ball, and then his right leg releases. He doesn't wind up, throw the ball, and fall back onto his right foot. Nor does he wind up, pick up his right leg, and then

> **Look for the Dirty Right Toe**
>
> If you see a player with a dirty right toe, take him for a partner. Don't bet against him. Chances are he's a long hitter, because this tells you he has a good right leg release.

throw the ball. The pitcher is allowing the right leg to follow and go with the flow of the action. The point is that as a golfer you're better to be late with the action (release of your right leg) than early. If you are early, it's out of sync and it doesn't work.

Leg Action Exercise: Width of Stance

The general rule is to have your feet about shoulder width apart. That is, the outside of the feet should be even with the outside of your shoulders.

Here is a way to find your personal width while doing the leg action exercise. When your right knee goes to the target and you are holding your finish, if the right knee has passed the left knee, then your stance is too narrow. If there is a gap or daylight between your right and left knees, your stance is too wide.

What is closer to the ideal position is when your left and right thighs are even with each other. You'll see no gap between the legs, and the right knee hasn't gone past the left knee. Being in this position helps you to have your weight posted over your left shoelace as you hold your finish and allows you to be in balance with your weight on your left side.

Timing of Right Knee Turn

Let's look at the timing of the right knee going toward the target. You know how a marionette puppet works when you pull a string on its hand—the hand comes up in the air. If I tie a string to the pad of your glove hand and tie the other end of the string to your right knee, here's what happens. When your glove swings through the ball, the string is loose. But when you pull your glove hand through the ball, the string becomes tight at the four o'clock position. The glove hand goes up into the finish and pulls the right knee toward the target. Imagine this being the cause of the right knee going toward the target. Your right knee can travel no faster than your glove hand. Again, you are better off late than early with this.

Concentrate on taking care of striking the ball first, and then allow the right knee to go with the flow of the glove hand into the finish. Start with slow, comfortable swings. Swing your glove hand into a finish position with the butt of the club toward the target like a barrel on a gun. Now as you hold your finish, your right knee will also point toward the target. PGA Tour player Scott Hoch suggests that you try to visualize at this moment an arrow going through your right knee, pointing toward the target. As you hold your finish you have two checkpoints toward the target:

103

1. The butt of your club is pointing toward your target like a barrel on a gun.

2. Your right knee is toward the target, and you should feel that the entire right leg is relaxed and comfortable.

You have arrived as a golfer when you have the feeling that your entire right side was pulled through by your left side.

Help Yourself

It is very important for you to learn this finish position. By practicing the same exact motion repeatedly, you'll gain muscle memory. Each time you make a golf swing, hold your finish position and ask yourself, "Where am I?" If you are not quite in the right position,

Allow the right knee to follow the flow of the glove hand into the finish.

take the time, while you are holding your finish, to adjust your body so you feel what is correct. Then, next time try to swing into that position. If you take the time to practice the two finish checkpoints, it will not be very long before you are automatically swinging into this target-oriented position. By repeating a full finish with every swing, good timing will come to you sooner rather than later.

How to Check Your Finish Position

As I have said, a golf swing takes a little more than a second to complete. When you make contact with the ball, you are in the middle of your swing. Try to keep your eyes focused on impact until your glove hand is in the finish position. While you are holding your finish, check your right knee. When your right knee is toward the target in the cor-

The author demonstrates a good finish. The right knee is toward the target and the right leg is relaxed.

105

rect position, rotate your head without raising it to check that the butt of your club is pointing toward the target. By not picking up your head to look, you are helping yourself to maintain your spine angle, and you are also on your way to becoming more target-aware and more precise with your total body movement.

Ideally, you don't want your lower body to get too aggressive, and equally as important, you don't want it to hold back too much. When the sequence and timing are correct, the right leg releases and goes with the flow. The lower body is solid at impact and causes no resistance to the swing as you follow through.

It is an old pro trick: if you want the ball to go to the right, be more aggressive with your lower body. If you know the lower body positions and can duplicate them, you will eliminate a reason for a slice. Being more quiet with your lower body will help you to make more solid contact with the ball.

In the next chapter we will aim the body, putting you into a stance that will enable you to react to the target with precision in each swing. Your stance sets your swing plane in position and is an important ingredient for your swing to be able to repeat itself.

Tournament Player Advice

NBC Golf anchorman and great pro Johnny Miller once told me that he learned something from another great pro, Gary Player. He was watching Gary hit balls, and it appeared to him that as Gary returned to impact, he was trying to duplicate or simulate where he began. There was no early exaggeration of leg action. "This helped to create a strong left side to hit against, which added the feeling of having a solid base, and allowed me to keep my swing plane in position."

PGA Tour player Billy Mayfair says, "I favor the weight just a bit on the inside edges of my shoes. I try to stay balanced over my shoelaces. The thing I think most about over my shots is to keep equal balance."

6

POWER STANCE: LAY YOUR FOUNDATION

Stance and alignment provide stability and aim for the golf swing. Learn the correct setup and you will hit the ball farther and straighter. As Masters champion Ben Crenshaw said, "All the pros are continually working on fine-tuning their aim on a daily basis. They have to have themselves in the proper position before they swing the club."

The game of golf has been described as a walk through a well-manicured park with something to do—bump the ball around. With a precise, fundamentally sound golf swing, you are target shooting in a big outdoor arena.

To shoot at a target, you must understand how best to position your body to get the results you want. This is called *alignment*. The dictionary defines alignment as the proper positioning or state of adjustment of parts in relation to each other.

Alignment: Be Target-Aware

To align yourself correctly, first make yourself target-aware. Stand behind your ball about ten feet, in a direct line with your target. Visualize a straight line running from your target through your ball to where you are standing. Think of your target as twelve o'clock in the field.

When you take your stance, lay a club in front of your toes and have that club pointing slightly right of your target. This sets your toe line in a position that favors an inside-out swing. Your body alignment is now in what is referred to as a slightly closed stance, which is in line with your desired swing path.

After you have addressed the ball, always check that your hips are consistent with your toe line. You can check this by taking your stance and laying a club across your hips. This line should also be parallel with your toe line. This will help you gain the feeling of your hips

The author with songwriter Chuck Jackson working on alignment. Your toe line should point slightly right of your target.

working together with your feet and legs in the setup. Check your shoulders with the same method as your hips. Lay a club across your shoulders to see if they are aligned slightly right of your target or close to one o'clock in the field, along with your hips and feet. The alignment of the body requires that the shoulders, hips, and feet are all parallel lines in relation to your swing path.

Slightly Closed Stance

Again, the body position that you want—to produce the power draw—is a slightly closed stance. How you stand dictates the flow of your swing plane. When your golf swing has the proper fundamental mechanics, then how you aim yourself enables you to put the type of spin on the ball that you want. Learn first how to stand up to the target to flight your ball from right to left. This is a big step to better golf. This setup puts a spin on the ball that enables it to fly farther, roll farther, and be less affected by the wind.

This brings us to another example of golf being a game of opposites. To spin the ball to the left, you aim slightly to the right. Your arm swing follows your shoulder alignment.

Your body is aligned slightly toward one o'clock in the field. Your stance—which includes toe line, hip line, and shoulder line—favors one o'clock. Twelve o'clock is your primary target, but one o'clock is your secondary target. Here you have to be aware of human nature. Human nature tells us to react to the primary target. It takes practice and rehearsal to teach yourself to react to the secondary target. When you swing toward one o'clock, you swing up into the target, not across the target. This pattern gives you another piece that helps you to create your draw.

Swing Path

When I teach beginners and intermediate-level players, I prefer to teach the inside-to-out swing path. This is the power path. I have found that if you can position your feet, hips, and shoulders on this path, it will help your swing in three ways.

1. Your left shoulder is preset in a position that puts it closer to the ball, so it doesn't have as much distance to travel as you coil back.

2. As you reach your glove hand back to find your toe line, it will make it easier for you to swing back on an inside path.

3. Your arm swing follows your shoulder alignment. If your shoulders are aligned a bit to the right of the target, it will be easier for you to swing that way.

Key Elements of the Power Stance

Following is an outline of all the key elements of the power stance. These elements of positioning, alignment, balance, and relaxed preparedness for action are the foundation for a consistent and powerful swing.

Comfort

When you are comfortable as you stand over the ball, you are ready to begin your swing. Your body is whiplike and will not cause the many swing flaws attributed to tension. Body comfort at address is the first step to distance and accuracy.

Width of Stance

Remember the general rule is that you should stand with your feet near shoulder width apart. That is, the outside of the feet are even with the outside of your shoulders. This is close to your normal balanced standing position. Here is an exception—notice the tour players. Their stance is slightly wider with the driver, because the lower body is the support or base of the swing and with the driver you have a more full swing arc. Your clubhead speed can exceed 110 miles per hour. If you are a pro, a wider stance or base will help you support that bigger arc and aid in balance while your clubhead flies through impact.

Weight Distribution

Feel equal weight on both feet, favoring the weight a little on the inside edges of your shoes. You can do this by giving yourself a comfortable, knock-kneed feeling so slight that you feel it yet it is unnoticeable to the eye. Feel 45 percent of your weight on your heels and 55 percent of your weight near the balls of your feet. Here again you are close to even, but you have 10 percent more of your weight forward.

You feel catlike in a ready position. Stand in a solid, comfortable position so that if someone gave you a nudge from any direction you

Foot Position

Your left foot should be flared slightly toward your target. There is a very good reason for this. In this position as you swing full speed through the impact area and into the finish, you will not put pressure on your left knee, and your left heel will be in a bit from perpendicular. Think of your instep as being in the neighborhood of 20 to 40 degrees open to your swing path. The right foot can be slightly flared out or straight depending on what works best for you.

would be able to keep your balance. You should feel as though you are in a good athletic position, ready to move in any direction.

Knee Flex

What you want here is just enough flex so there is no tension in the knee area. The knee flex in a golf swing is close to your normal standing position. A slight, comfortable flex is ideal. Too much flex creates tension, and straight-legged, locked knees create tension as well, so avoid these extremes.

Spine Angle

To get the proper spine angle, bend forward from the waist as if you were going to touch your toes. Once your head and spine are tilted

The author and Chuck Jackson working on balance. Stand in a good athletic position, ready to move in any direction.

close to 20 degrees, your upper body is leaning forward so that your arms hang freely from your shoulders. You should be able to swing your arms back and forth comfortably from this position. Here's a tip: Sam Snead once told Ben Crenshaw that to get the relaxed arm feeling, think of your arms hanging down as if oil was dripping from your shoulders.

Glove Hand Position

As you stand over the ball and are ready to swing, a good general rule is to position the last three fingers of your glove hand off of the inside of your left thigh. You do not want your hands behind the ball or outside of your left thigh. This seems like a simple point, but new players are many times unaware of the correct position.

113

Tour player Tom Purtzer demonstrates correct position at address.

The Fist

Here is a tip that has been around for a while. It has to do with how far you stand from the ball. When you are in your good golf posture and standing over the ball as if ready to swing, take your right hand off the club and make a fist. Your fist should fit between the butt of your club and your left thigh. The fist distance should be the same regardless of the length of the club in your hand. Some individuals will have a fist and a thumb, and that is also close enough. Always be aware of and try for the same measurement.

By showing the same space each time, your glove hand can now travel on the same path in relation to your body no matter which club you are using. This gives you a guide to avoid reaching out too far away from your body to make the shot. Here's a caution—players that reach out too far are placed in a position that is impossible to swing inside-out from. If you see players reaching as they stand over a ball, you can bet they are going to slice the ball. Reaching out also takes

114

Your fist should fit between the butt of your club and your left thigh at address, regardless of the length of the club in your hand. Avoid reaching out too far from your body to make a shot.

you away from your comfortable position with arms hanging down freely. The result of reaching is that you create tension in your arms, and any tension anywhere in your body during the swing has proven itself to be the real foe of accuracy and distance.

Be correct, be comfortable. Bend enough at the waist that your arms hang down freely from your shoulders. Then notice if your hands are near a fist's width in front of the inside area of your left thigh. This will improve your ability to swing inside-out and hit the ball up to your full potential distance.

Head Position

Tilt the top of your head just a bit to the right. I tell my students to think of a pillow on their right shoulder. Head position is important because your head has weight. By tilting it to the right you are presetting it so you will be able to move comfortably and fully extend into the backswing. We also want the weight behind the ball on the backswing, so now we can have all the weight coming through the ball.

Keep your chin up. If your chin is too close to your chest, as your left shoulder swings back, it will cause your head to go out of position. The same thing will happen as you swing through, because the right shoulder will push the head too far forward. You want to keep your head from going up and down or too far back and forth. With the chin up you will also create a straighter spine angle, which helps you to coil the upper body. Have your chin up enough that you are looking down at the ball over your cheekbones. Feel the back of the neck a bit wrinkled. You could also have the chin up enough so that you could see the ball through your nostrils—if that were possible. The key is not to let the head fall too far forward. Keep in mind that the head is a sensitive balancing weight for the entire swing. The more still you can keep your head, the faster and smoother your swing will be. Also a still head contributes to your swing staying in the position that you envision and desire.

Right Arm

Allow your right arm to relax. Concentrate and practice right arm relaxation. Your right elbow will be in closer to your body than your left. This helps you to establish a slightly closed stance. With this stance, your swing plane is positioned a bit to the right of the target. When you swing on path, on plane with your clubface looking at the target, your ball will have a resulting draw spin. Also, having the relaxed right elbow in helps you to be able to go into the backswing on an inside path.

Body Alignment

To help create a draw, your toe line will be just a little right of your target. This slightly closed stance favors one o'clock in the field. Your hips and your shoulders should be even with your toe line. By setting yourself in this position, you have aligned your swing plane and swing path to create the draw spin on the ball.

Ball Position

Most great players will tell you to position the ball opposite the inside of your left heel with the general swing. Playing the ball in only one spot helps your timing. You get used to it there and you get a feeling for reacting to it there. Get good with the ball being in this position first. Specialty shots are an exception: an example would be the driver (in nonwindy conditions the ball will be played a bit more forward).

Major Flaw: Open Shoulders

Here is a caution. One of the major flaws among average golfers is that their shoulders are usually open to their stance line and pointing

Position the ball opposite the inside of your left heel with the general swing. Playing the ball in only one spot helps your timing.

toward an eleven o'clock position. Open shoulders inhibit the inside swing takeaway on the backswing and cause an improper weight position during the transition from backswing to downswing. This forces the golfer to swing on an outside-to-inside swing path. The most usual result is the dreaded slice, an affliction suffered by 80 percent of all golfers. Even Tiger Woods had a tendency to be a little open with his shoulders.

Take Aim

Correct grip alignment is a detail that needs to be examined each and every swing. Hold the club straight out in front of you with your left hand and arm. The bottom edge of the club should be perpendicular to the ground or a hair to the left. Look at the "V" formed between your left thumb and forefinger. It should be pointing between your neck and right shoulder. You should be as careful and detailed as top tour players are with their glove hand and clubhead relationship—it should be the same every time.

Also, think of the backswing as part of your aim. Compare the backswing to the archer who slowly pulls the arrow back a moment before releasing. He then takes final aim to make sure the arrow flies true to the target.

Proper alignment will not cure all that ails you, but this ingredient is crucial to a good swing and it is a big step to becoming a better player. By keeping your body in relaxed control during your swing, you will discover power and accuracy.

Good aim and good swing mechanics enable you to send your ball along the intended flight that you have visualized. In the next chapter we are finally ready to go to the driving range and exercise your golf swing.

Tournament Player Advice

PGA Tour player, Senior PGA Tour player, and past PGA Tour commissioner Deane Beaman: "Alignment is critical to any golf swing, it's the key. You can't hit it where you want unless you have good aim."

PGA Tour player Tom Purtzer: "I think it's important to spend time and go over a checklist to make sure everything is in the right spot before you start the club back. If you are not set up properly, chances are you are not going to hit a very good shot."

PGA Tour player Mike Reid: "The most important part of the golf swing for the Tour player is the preparation for the swing, the alignment and the setup. I love the detail of being meticulous."

7

NATURAL RHYTHM: BALANCE, TEMPO, AND TIMING

The golf swing requires balance as well as tempo, timing, and rhythm. Work on this relationship and swing to the beat. Tempo, timing, and rhythm transform a mechanical, fundamentally sound swing into one smooth action—poetry in motion.

Balance: Key to Becoming a Good Player

Balance is the key to becoming a good player. I'm talking about balance in the finish position. If you are sloppy in your finish position, then something was not right coming through the ball.

Two areas of concentration will help you balance. First, keep your head still when you are going through the ball and into the finish. When your head is still, with your eyes focused on the ground where your ball used to be as you swing your glove hand into the finish, it

119

is easier to keep your upper body weight between your two feet, resulting in better balance.

A second aid to help you achieve better balance is to hold your finish. Being able to hold the finish with upper body weight between the two feet is the trademark of all great ball strikers. Your golf club becomes a balancing instrument. It's like a circus performer on the high wire. To maintain balance, the performer holds onto a long balancing pole.

Your golf club is your long pole. Most of the weight of the golf club is in the clubhead. To balance while holding your finish position, make sure your glove hand stays firm and in control. You should feel that your glove hand is using your club to maintain balance. Your glove hand is on the target side of your body and the weight of the club is on the other side, thus acting as a counterbalance. This image is helpful in four ways:

120

1. You have something to hold on to for balance.

2. Your grip pressure stays consistent all the way through the ball and up into the finish.

3. It encourages a complete swing each time.

4. It gives you a finish position that you can feel and repeat.

Golf legend Arnold Palmer agrees that visualizing the club like a balancing pole "has merit." The result is a full finish which increases

Dan Forsman on Balance
PGA Tour winner Dan Forsman: "Balance is important to a good swing. You need the proper weight transfer. You want to try for body movement back and body movement through to a well-balanced finish. The balancing pole tip is a good idea. It makes a lot of sense."

your swing arc, and that means more clubhead speed through the ball. You will hit it farther.

How important is holding your finish? PGA Tour player Keith Clearwater says, "In all my golf clinics I teach one thing to all amateurs. It is, in my opinion, the one ingredient in the golf swing that will improve a player at all levels the fastest. It is holding your finish.

"I make them hold their finish until the ball comes to a rest. That implants such a positive image in their minds. After you make a swing, if you top it and it rolls four inches, you watch poised as it rolls and rolls and trickles to a stop. No matter what, learn to hold that finish all the way. Get that discipline because it will carry over into a lot of other things." Keep these thoughts on a balanced finish position and your swing will also have a more full swing arc, which translates into more power.

Now before we move on to tempo, timing, and rhythm, let's review a good balanced finish position. Your head is still and there is a slight arch in the back as a result. The weight is on the left foot and the right knee is pointing toward the target. The right toe helps as a balance point, but at the top of the finish there is significantly less weight on it. The right leg is relaxed and comfortable. The butt of the club points toward the target and the golf shaft is parallel to the ground. The glove hand is using the golf club at this moment as a balancing instrument. Having balance in your finish suggests that you controlled the clubhead speed. If you lose your balance it could indicate that you were simply swinging beyond your control limit. (See the photos on pages 34, 38, and 44.)

121

Tempo, Timing, and Rhythm

Hale Irwin, Craig Stadler, Corey Pavin, and Tom Purtzer, among others, have all stated that the most important part of a golf swing is repeatability, or tempo, timing, and rhythm. As a teacher, when I originate a swing concept and have the opportunity to get feedback from great stars of the game, then I have a valuable key to pass on to my students. In this section I will pass on to you some of these thoughts related to timing.

Backswing Pace: Go Slow and Stop on the Dime

Tempo is the rate of speed. First, what rate of speed do you want going into the backswing? Remember, Bobby Jones, the world's greatest golfer, said, "I never saw anyone go back too slow."

What happens if your rate of speed on the backswing is too fast?

1. The speed can lift your body up as you go up and into the transition area where you start back down. It takes you out of your swing and changes your spine angle.

2. You lose the feel of where you are—the more slowly you go back, the more you can feel your correct position.

3. When you make the transition from backswing to downswing, speed makes you jerky, you lose the smoothness, and at that moment you are out of control.

4. Too much speed going back means too much speed coming down, and that can cause your body to lower and is one reason for a fat shot.

5. A fast backswing under pressure only has one way to go—too fast—and you are out of control.

Here's a story from my early days as a teaching pro. I've known many hustlers that would go to the driving range and watch people practice and would then approach, in a friendly manner, the golfer with the fastest backswing. The hustler knows if you have a fast backswing, you have lack of control. The hustler knows that playing for money makes certain people nervous, and they get anxious and their backswing gets too fast.

If you have a fast backswing, you will appear to a hustler to have a big flashing neon sign over your head that says, "Pigeon, Pigeon." All because the hustler knows he can get you out of control and take your money. Keep the hustlers away, go slow.

Another way to think of being able to slow into the backswing is to compare it to stopping on a dime in the driveway with your left front car tire. If I told you that I'd give you ten thousand dollars if you could stop that tire exactly on that dime, I bet you would lean your head out of the window and go very slowly, park deliberately on the dime, and say, "Give me the money." I doubt very much you would step on the gas, speed up to the dime, and then jam on the brakes. Well, that is like what some unschooled golfers do. What you should do is think of your glove hand as the car and the top of the backswing as the spot where the dime is. So go up slowly, get the dime, and then come down—a slow backswing will help you to be the one playing better golf.

Downswing Pace: Freeway On-Ramp or Loaded Gun

Let's compare this, again, to getting on the freeway. The downswing is the freeway ramp. Your speed builds up gradually, but you're not on the freeway yet. As your glove hand is coming down from your left shoulder ball-and-socket joint (for right-handed players), it reaches a point at which it is no longer coming down (seven o'clock) and it picks up the swing path to go through the impact area. It is at this time that you are on the freeway, and it's now time to put pedal to the metal. Step on the gas and accelerate your glove hand through the ball and into the finish.

The second example is to think of a gun. When you pause at the top of the backswing and everything is set up properly, you have a loaded gun. As you bring your club down, controlling it with your glove hand, the speed gradually increasing, at seven o'clock you are ready to fire—now pull the trigger. When your glove hand picks up the swing path, that is the time to pull the trigger. Rotate, then accelerate your glove hand through the ball and into the finish.

The more glove hand pulling speed you can generate through the ball and into the finish, the more clubhead speed you'll have through impact. It's important to note here that you do not want the clubhead speed to control you. You must control the clubhead speed. Start slowly and gradually increase the speed so you can accelerate through the ball and into the finish and still maintain a well-balanced position.

Beware that clubhead speed translates into centrifugal force. This force wants to pull your head along as you swing into the finish. Don't let it. Always try to maintain your head position. Also, don't get tight with the right hand, as it will cost you distance and accuracy.

124

People tell me all the time that they can hit their irons but not their woods. Woods create greater centrifugal force. Try to keep your head still longer when swinging the longer clubs. Remember when practicing timing to build a racetrack before you race.

Greg Norman says, "Don't call me a natural." As you are going through the ball and into the finish, three natural things want to occur, and you must work against these natural tendencies:

1. For the unschooled golfer, the right hand and arm want to get too involved, causing you to jam through or hit at the ball, which causes your spine angle to lift. Keep your right arm relaxed.

2. It is natural to be curious. If this occurs through impact, your eyes and head lift up too soon and again your spine angle changes. When you work against human nature your golf swing will look natural and be more effective (another example of golf being a game of opposites). Keep your eyes on the impact point through the finish.

3. As humans we go with the flow. Now your clubhead is traveling 70 to 100 m.p.h. through the ball and up into the finish. The clubhead speed translates into centrifugal force. This force can also lift you out of your swing. Use the club as a balancing pole to maintain your balance.

Rhythm

Rhythm is movement characterized by a regular recurrence of beats. A great example is given by Sam Snead: compare the rhythm of a golf swing to a waltz. Start back slowly, pause at the top (one beat), come

PGA Tour player Lanny Wadkins fighting the force—the centrifugal force of the clubhead that can lift you out of your swing. Note his glove hand and club shaft position sliding up on the glass wall.

down slowly, and gradually increase your speed. When your glove hand picks up the swing path at seven o'clock (your through-swing), pick up the beat and increase it up into the finish. Maybe you can think of a tune you like and fit the beat to your swing.

Emotions can change your tempo, timing, and rhythm. During a round of golf you can feel many different emotions that can change your adrenaline level. Adrenaline can help your golf swing, as PGA Tour player Bruce Lietzke has said, and it can hurt your swing. On a scale of 1 to 10 (10 being too excited), Lietzke tries to maintain a level between 5 and 7. This helps you to maintain a more even tempo. When you maintain this harmony, you'll shoot better numbers.

Tempo, timing, and rhythm transform a mechanical swing into one smooth action. If you practice good fundamentals and practice a repeating golf swing, timing will come to you and you will notice that your percentage of good shots increases.

Practice to Increase Your Percentage

In practice, the 7-iron is the first club you want to get good with. I recommend that you use a tee in the beginning, when you are practicing an improved swing. This keeps your attention on the action of your body, and not on the ground or surface the ball sits on. Also, it's a good idea to get good at hitting the ball off a tee because, during a round, you'll have eighteen tee shots. I'd suggest that in the beginning you only hit a small or medium bucket of balls at a time—fifty to seventy balls. This allows you to start and finish fresh. If you hit too many balls at one time, your muscles can get fatigued and then your mechanics will get sloppy. Most good players practice two or three times a week.

When I work with students, before they go out with their 7-iron, I use it and measure the distance from their toe line to the ball. I do

Tempo Tips from the Ladies Tour

After you have the fundamentals of a good golf swing, tempo becomes the most important part. Here's what some of the most talented players on the Ladies Tour have to say about tempo.

LPGA Tour star Cindy Rarick: "Controlling the speed of my backswing is my major swing thought. You don't hit the ball on the backswing, so take it slow and you'll create more torque, and that translates into power."

LPGA star Hollis Stacy: "Take it back slow. Practice taking it back slow on the practice tee, because it tends to get quicker on the golf course. I'd also like amateurs to always maintain a positive attitude and don't be too hard on yourselves. Accept that you're human. There will be mistakes but keep going forward."

Tour player Kate Hughes: "To me, tempo is a matter of the whole body turning back together and coming through together toward the target and into the finish. Compare it to a gymnast in the Olympics. How do they end up? They just stick the finish. I time it going back and try to come through and stick my finish in a balanced position. . . . In addition, keep in mind that emotions and pressure situations can change tempo. I try to stay in control with what I call cool confidence. If you get too excited, think quiet mind, quiet body. Take a deep breath and relax your shoulders before the shot."

President of the LPGA Judy Dickinson: "Here's my tip for amateurs to get better tempo: Sometimes I hum songs—the "Tennessee Waltz" is a good one [just like Sam Snead]. Sometimes I do a slow count. Take it back slow and give yourself a slight pause at the top. It's not easy but it keeps you from being way too quick. Pressure makes you quicker, so keep it slow on the backswing and you'll always have more control!"

this so when they practice, they know that they are standing the same distance from the ball as they were during their lessons. I recommend that you do the same to make sure that you are positioning yourself consistently for every shot.

Swing easy to begin with. Start by swinging slowly, gradually picking up the speed through the ball and into the finish. As you swing faster, always work for a good balanced finish position.

Once you reach the point of being able to hit 70 percent of shots well, the next step I recommend is to go through the same process with your 5-iron. If you are good with your 5-iron, you'll be good with your 6-iron and, if you're good with your 7-iron, you'll be good with your 8-iron, 9-iron, and wedge. So just by getting good with two clubs, the 5-iron and the 7-iron, you'll actually be getting good with six clubs.

The next step is to get good with your 5-wood. Practice with it until you hit 70 percent of the fairways. This could take some time,

Tournament Player Advice

PGA Tour player Mike Reid, the player nicknamed "Radar" for the accuracy of his shots: "There's no substitute for practice. There is plenty of room out there for that little ball and you don't necessarily have to swing perfectly."

PGA Tour player Hal Sutton: "I want a fundamentally sound repeating swing. During practice I focus on being consistent. To get quicker results, practice is the key. Here's a tip: you'll have a good golf swing if you can get the arms, the big muscles in your back, and your legs to move together simultaneously."

Senior PGA Tour player Dewitt Weaver: "Practice helps you stay focused when the pressure is on."

maybe six months to a year, but taking the time to do it right will pay off for you because accuracy is what is important. Use your 5-wood as your driver until you get 70 percent good with it. If you don't take time to make friends with your 5-wood, then your 3-wood and driver will always be difficult to hit.

The Cutting Edge

Never be intimidated by the surface that your ball sits on. If you are pulling through with your muscles on the left side, your golf club will work for you. The bottom edge of your irons is like the cutting edge of a mower. It is designed to cut through the ground or the grass. Remember the ground is made up of particles. It will give, even if your ball is on hard dirt.

You could take an old club and hit a golf ball off of cement. This can result in sparks, but if you are pulling through properly you'll never hurt yourself. Those players who push with their right hand will suffer from impact vibration and in time will need medical attention. In this case the club is pushed into the ground and then has no place to go. It will stop abruptly. Pull through to take advantage of the cutting edge of your irons.

Tournament Player Advice

PGA and Senior PGA Tour star Miller Barber: "Don't put pressure on yourself by worrying about the other players. Play the course. If you beat the golf course, you'll be a contender."

Bobby Jones, the world's greatest golfer: "Your only opponent is old man par."

Traditional Values of Golf

Throughout your round you are practicing self-control, patience, concentration, etiquette, courtesy, and sportsmanship. The basic human values of kindness, consideration, and respect are a major part of the traditional values of golf. Here are the thoughts of some of the game's most respected players:

Deane Beaman: "Golf has the pure essence of sportsmanship, the fact that you respect your fellow competitor and the fact that you respect the rules of the game and you know that you don't gain value by violating the rules. This is so important and one of the reasons why golf is so popular."

Ben Crenshaw: "We have a game that has lasted five hundred years, and one of the simple constants is it is a very congenial game. It is one of the last endeavors where you are expected to act like a lady or gentleman. There is no other game that fosters friendship like golf, there is no other game that knits the generations better than golf, but it still retains a very simple idea, to get the ball in the hole in the fewest amount of strokes regardless of what clubs you are playing with. The thought of the game is always fresh every day. All of these reasons and more are the fabric of tradition."

Gary Player: "Playing golf is the greatest lesson that one can learn in life. This game teaches strength of mind, humility, patience, courage. No college, Harvard or Princeton, teaches you like golf. Learn the rules, learn the etiquette and practice and play and you will be rewarded by the traditional values."

Practice for Success

Make friends with all of the clubs in your bag through practice. You don't want to carry around a bag full of strangers. Practice and get confidence with all of the clubs in your bag.

Some people compare a golf swing to a choreographed dance step. The word *practice* can have a tedious connotation. Another way to think about it is that you are going out to exercise your swing, or rehearse the precision of the swinging action.

Chuck Jackson's road to improvement is a good example of the benefits of practice. Chuck, the younger brother of Reverend Jesse Jackson, started taking lessons from me three years ago at age forty-two. He had never played golf before that time. After eighteen lessons and six months he went from a 23 handicap to an 11 handicap.

At age forty-five Chuck is playing to a 6 handicap using my winning instruction formula. Practice is the operative word to achieve this success. Chuck hit three hundred balls a day, five days a week, for the first six months. He hit approximately thirty balls per club, starting with the pitching wedge and then the 9-iron, 8-iron, and so on. However, Chuck hit very few drivers until after the first six months. He devoted twenty minutes to putting during each practice session.

Chuck came to golf at a time when he wanted to improve his lifestyle and have something to take the place of smoking. He will tell you that the cost of the game is nothing compared to the improvement of his physical and mental approach to life. I am confident that you, too, will reap the benefits of this traditional game, as have players through time and throughout the world.

AFTERWORD

I hope these lessons have given you a pattern or road map to follow so your mind and muscles are on the same track. If I have helped your thinking, your imagination, and your ability to visualize and feel your swing, then this book has accomplished its goal.

Keep in mind that golf is like life. Life has its ups and downs, but the more you are around, the more you learn. No matter how great you are at whatever age, your golf swing will always be a work in progress. At age sixty-five, Arnold Palmer told me, "I'm still learning."

Remember that well-schooled golfers properly position their body to the target, correctly aiming in the direction they want their ball to fly. They trust their swing by knowing it.

I wish you the best of success. Enjoy your swing as you grow and develop as a golf player.

Nancy Lopez on Persistence

Hall of Fame player Nancy Lopez says, "I want to be remembered as someone who never gave up on a golf course."

INDEX